GROWING

CONIFERS

Four-season
Plants

R. William Thomas

Susan F. Martin

& Kim Tripp

Guest Editors

FOR THE
ADVANCE
MENT OF
BOTANY
AND THE
SERVICE OF
THE CITY

BROOKLYN
BOTANIC
GARDEN
PUBLICATIONS
· MCMXCVII ·

Janet Marinelli
SERIES EDITOR

Beth Hanson
MANAGING EDITOR

Carol Goodstein
ASSOCIATE EDITOR

Bekka Lindstrom
ART DIRECTOR

Stephen K-M. Tim
VICE PRESIDENT, SCIENCE, LIBRARY & PUBLICATIONS

Judith D. Zuk
PRESIDENT

Elizabeth Scholtz
DIRECTOR EMERITUS

Handbook #152

Copyright © Autumn 1997 by the Brooklyn Botanic Garden, Inc.

Handbooks in the 21st-Century Gardening Series, formerly Plants & Gardens,

are published quarterly at 1000 Washington Ave., Brooklyn, NY 11225.

Subscription included in Brooklyn Botanic Garden subscriber membership dues ($35.00 per year).

ISSN # 0362-5850 ISBN # 1-889538-02-7

Printed by Science Press, a division of the Mack Printing Group

Table of Contents

Four-season Plants

BY R. WILLIAM THOMAS

Conifers provide gardens with strong form, color and texture in every season and come in an array of shapes other than the ubiquitous pyramid.

CONIFERS ARE THE MOST UNDERRATED plants in the landscape world. For many people, a conifer is merely a Christmas tree or a blue spruce in the front yard. Landscape professionals fall in one of two camps in their regard for conifers: the staunch enthusiasts who tend to establish collections or the downright contemptuous who erroneously believe that designing with conifers is inherently difficult. This book is intended to persuade gardeners otherwise.

Conifers offer more than winter interest. They provide the garden with strong form, color and texture in *every* season. From towering trees to spreading shrubs and rambling ground covers, they come in an array of shapes —not just the ubiquitous pyramid. Colors include not only umpteen shades of green but also yellows, blues and, in winter, maroons. Some conifers retain one color throughout the year, while others change dramatically, with foliage going from brilliant yellow in the spring to green for the remainder of the year. Before their needles drop in autumn, deciduous conifers turn rich yellows and oranges. Conifer textures can be as bold as a ponderosa pine or as soft and fine as a shore juniper.

Correctly chosen and placed, conifers fit most definitions of "low maintenance." Established plants require little care and, unlike perennials, need no dividing or deadheading. And these versatile, four-season plants form the structure and backbone of our gardens. Conifers can divide space into garden rooms, block unattractive views and focus attention on specimen plants, sculptures or special vistas.

Conifers have interesting histories, too. At 2,000 to 4,000 years old, bristlecone pines and giant sequoias are among the world's oldest living plants. Dwarfed, 1,000-year-old eastern arborvitaes have been found growing on cliffs in Ontario, Canada. Dawn redwoods were thought to be long extinct until living plants were found in China in the 1940s. Fossils indicate that the species was once widespread throughout North America and Asia. Recent headlines announced the sensational discovery of not just a species, but a whole new genus — Wollemi pine (*Wollemia nobilis*) — only 100 miles from Sydney, Australia.

When designing your garden, think first of the four-season plants. They are the ones that will set the stage for every day of the year. Consult this handbook to help you identify, grow and design with conifers and to learn some of the best species available. Use conifers as major trees, hedges, shrubs and ground covers. Think of them as familiar, useful and attractive garden plants rather than simply as specimens for a collection. Mix them with perennials, use them as backgrounds for flowering trees and shrubs and plant them in containers for year-round interest. Plant them and the world will be a better place!

Conifer Names

BY R. WILLIAM THOMAS

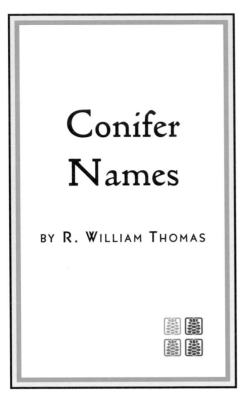

THROUGHOUT THIS handbook you'll find conifers identified by both common names, written in English, and scientific names, in Latin. Because the common names are easy to pronounce, most gardeners prefer them. Unfortunately, they can be confusing because many plants have several common names. To clear up the confusion, botanists adopted the binomial system 200 years ago. Each plant is identified by two names, the genus followed by a specific epithet. Both are italicized or underlined, and the first (genus) name is capitalized. Thus, the scientific name of the eastern white pine is *Pinus strobus*. If a species includes a variety, subspecies or cultivar, that name follows the species name.

A **genus** (genera, plural) is a group of plants that share some characteristics, such as similar leaves and cones. Species within the genus, however, may vary greatly. The genus *Juniperus*, for example, includes trees, shrubs and ground covers. All have evergreen foliage that is either scale-like or needle-like.

Members of a **species** share a number of characteristics. To the gardener, species names are important. If you want a fir tree, for instance, you would not order an *Abies* (the generic name for firs), because there are about 40 different kinds of fir. Instead, you would specify a species — *Abies concolor* (concolor or white fir), for example.

A **variety** retains the basic character of the species but has one or more distinctive characteristics of its own. For example, Douglas-fir (*Pseudotsuga men-*

Cedrus atlantica 'Pendula', above, and *C.a.* 'Glauca', right, are both cultivars of the Atlas cedar. One was selected for its dramatic drooping branches and the other for its intensely blue foliage.

ziesii) leaves typically are green, but a significant number of trees in the eastern part of the plant's range have bluish leaves. These are classified as *P. menziesii* var. *glauca* (blue Douglas-fir). A **subspecies** is very similar to a variety and is abbreviated "ssp." — for example, *Cedrus libani* ssp. *atlantica*. A **form** (or forma) is a minor genetic variant that occasionally occurs in the wild. It is abbreviated "f." — as in *Abies concolor* f. *argentea*.

A **cultivar** is a named selection that differs in some respect from other plants of its species. A cultivar exists only because people work to propagate it. For example, if one seedling in a field of eastern white pines is narrower than the rest, a nursery worker may choose to propagate it and name it *Pinus strobus* 'Upright', thereby selecting a new cultivar. Cultivar names are always capitalized, never written in italics, and are enclosed in single quotation marks.

A **hybrid** results from the crossing of two plant species, sometimes naturally but most often intentionally. Hybrids are noted with a multiplication sign (x). The symbol precedes the genus when the genus itself is a hybrid, such as X *Cupressocyparis leylandii,* a cross between *Cupressus macrocarpa* (Monterey cypress) and *Chamaecyparis nootkatensis* (Alaska-cedar). It goes after the genus if the species is a hybrid, such as *Taxus* x *media*, a cross between *T. cuspidata* and *T. baccata*. Cultivars are sometimes selected from hybrids.

Although species generally come true from seed, cultivars and hybrids usually need to be propagated asexually (by cuttings or grafts) to retain the desired characteristics.

CONIFERS ARE WOODY plants that include trees, shrubs and ground covers. They are typically evergreen. Conifers belong to a group of plants called gymnosperms, with exposed seeds that are usually, but not always, borne in cones.

This chapter is a basic guide to the various characteristics that distinguish one conifer from another. It points out major features and how they vary from conifer to conifer. For more detailed information on the characteristics of individual species and their cultivars, see the descriptions in the Encyclopedia of Conifers, beginning on page 39.

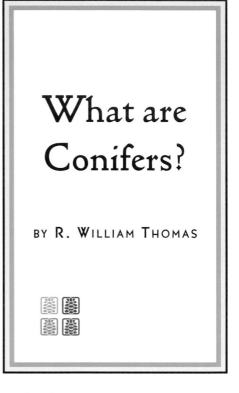

What are Conifers?

BY R. WILLIAM THOMAS

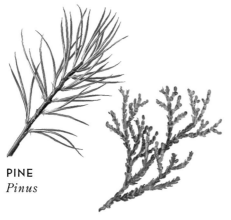

PINE
Pinus

ARBORVITAE
Thuja occidentalis

Conifer leaves are either needle-like, such as those of pine, or scale-like, such as those of arborvitae.

SHAPE

Conifers can be large trees, bushy shrubs or sprawling ground covers. Shape and size are often a plant's most obvious characteristics, but are not always reliable identifying features, because size doesn't always reflect age (see "What is a Dwarf Conifer?" page 11) and the habit of some plants changes as they mature.

LEAVES

Leaves can more accurately help determine the identity of a conifer. Check for the following characteristics:

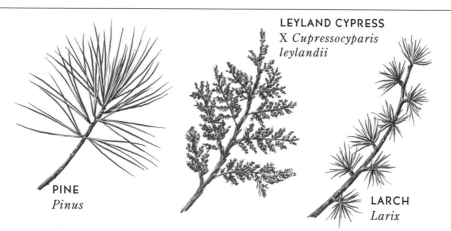

LEYLAND CYPRESS
X *Cupressocyparis
leylandii*

PINE
Pinus

LARCH
Larix

Observing how conifer leaves are attached to the stem is another way to distinguish one conifer from another. Leaves can be clustered, as in pine, flattened, as in Leyland cypress, or stalked, as in larch.

- Needle-like or scale-like
- Evergreen (most conifers) or deciduous (larch, for example)
- Size of the leaves
- How they are attached to the stem — flattened, stalked or clustered
- If clustered, how many leaves per cluster
- Shape of the leaf in cross-section — flat, as in firs, rounded, as in some pines, or quadrangular, as in spruce
- Color and markings (markings may be on the underside of the leaf). Be aware that blue leaves are the result of a white wax on the needle. The wax wears off with age and can be dissolved by oil sprays.

CONE OR FLESHY SEED

Although they're not always on the plant, cones and seeds are useful in identification. Some things to look for:

- Type of structure — typical cone, as in pine; berry-like cone, as in juniper; or fleshy, plum-like seed, as in *Cephalotaxus* (plum yew)

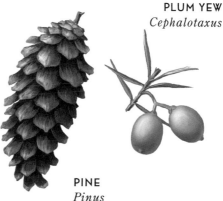

PLUM YEW
Cephalotaxus

PINE
Pinus

Conifers produce seeds in cones, or in the form of a fleshy seed.

9

CHAPTER 3

DOUGLAS-FIR
Pseudotsuga menziesii

PINE
Pinus

JAPANESE CEDAR
Cryptomeria

ARBORVITAE
Thuja

Cones come in all sizes and shapes, from the small cone of arborvitae to the large, woody cones of Douglas-fir and pine to the ball-shaped cone of the Japanese cedar.

- Size and color of cone; presence or absence of bracts (papery scales)
- Attachment to stem — upright or pendant
- Persistence, or how long it remains on the plant

Most conifer genera, including the pines, spruces, hemlocks and firs, are monoecious, meaning that they produce male and female cones on the same plant. A few genera, including yews, junipers and monkey puzzle trees, are dioecious and produce only male or female cones on an individual plant; in other words, in these genera, seeds are found only on female plants.

HEMLOCK
Tsuga

CEDAR
Cedrus

Conifers bear their cones either upright, as on cedar, or pendant, as on hemlock.

BARK, TWIGS & BUDS

Bark, twigs and buds can also help in identifying conifers, especially in differentiating species within a genus. Bark color can be brown, gray, green, red-orange or white. The texture of bark can be smooth, rough, plate-like, fis-

10

By some definitions, any conifer that at maturity is not as tall as its parent species is a dwarf. In other words, a plant that grows only 40 feet tall, when other plants of the parent species reach 80 feet, could be called a dwarf. But if you planted this "dwarf" next to your front door, you probably wouldn't be happy. To clear up the confusion, the American Conifer Society has attempted to standardize the terminology as follows:

Miniature conifer — Grows less than 3 inches per year. Size at age 10 to 15 years is 2 to 3 feet.

Dwarf conifer — Grows 3 to 6 inches per year. Size at age 10 to 15 years is 3 to 6 feet.

Intermediate conifer — Grows 6 to 12 inches per year. Size at age 10 to 15 years is 6 to 15 feet.

Large conifer — Grows 12 inches or more per year. Size at age 10 to 15 years is greater than 15 feet.

Dwarf conifers originate as seedling or bud mutations. A seedling mutation is a seedling that is different from its fellow seedlings. A bud mutation occurs on an established plant and results in a branch that is different from the rest of the plant. Bud mutations may develop witches' brooms, a major source of dwarf conifers. These multi-branched, bushy offshoots with short branches and needles will, if successfully propagated, produce a compact plant. If this new plant turns out to be attractive and useful for the garden, it may then be given a cultivar name.

sured or exfoliating. It is important to note that on some plants, bark characteristics change with age. For example, the lacebark pine has smooth, greenish gray bark as a young plant. As the tree ages, the bark splits, peels and takes on a number of different colors, including brown, gray-green and white.

When observing buds, note the size and the presence of hairs or resin, and whether the shape is pointed or rounded.

With twigs, check whether they are smooth, hairy or ridged and are a specific color. Twigs look the same throughout the life of a plant; new growth on a hundred-year-old pine is the same as that on a five-year-old specimen.

Selecting Conifers for Your Garden

BY KIM TRIPP

E GARDENERS HAVE the best chance for success if we choose plants suited to our climates and the particular conditions in our gardens. Fortunately, there are plenty of delightful conifers for every garden from coast to coast. The following are some important factors to keep in mind when selecting conifers. See the Encyclopedia of Conifers, page 39, for specific information on each plant's "preference" for soil type, moisture, light, cold hardiness and so on.

TEMPERATURE

Gardeners tend to focus on cold hardiness as the single determinant of whether a plant is an appropriate choice for their properties. However, referring to the widely used USDA Plant Hardiness Zone Map, which is based on average annual minimum temperatures, is only a first step. In order to thrive, a long-lived plant must be well-adapted to seasonal extremes of heat as well as cold, and also to other patterns of temperature variation throughout the year, such as the duration of the extremes, and the accompanying moisture and other conditions.

Although most conifers are evergreen, there are dormant or quiescent periods when there is little or no active growth. In general, plants are far more tolerant of temperature extremes during a dormant or quiescent period than during active growth. For example, a prolonged period of extreme winter cold is much less likely to damage northern populations of balsam firs than an extended period of extreme summer heat because they are not actively growing in winter.

Keep in mind, too, that individuals of a species with a wide natural distribution may vary in hardiness. For instance, Douglas-fir is native from the mild Pacific Coast to the harsher Dakotas. Plants grown from seed collected in the western part of the range will likely be less cold- and drought-tolerant than those grown from more eastern sources. If possible, gardeners should be aware of the origin, or provenance, of these species, although unfortunately this information is rarely available.

Because roots are far more susceptible to temperature extremes than above-ground plant parts, below-ground temperatures are another consideration, especially when choosing conifers for containers, where the roots will be subjected to greater tem-

The cold-hardiness of individuals of a species with a wide distribution like Douglas-fir may vary. Try to learn the origin, or provenance, of these plants.

perature fluctuations than they would be in the ground (see "Conifers for Containers," page 22).

MACROCLIMATE AND MICROCLIMATE

Macroclimate describes the general characteristics of a region, such as annual precipitation, temperature range, daylength and regional trends in soil types. Microclimate describes the specific characteristics found in smaller areas of a region, or in a garden — a poorly drained corner, a sudden slope, a pocket of sandy soil in a clay basin, an especially windy inner city corridor, or the south side of a building, for example. When you choose conifers, keep in mind that cold air flows downhill and pools in low places, while hot air tends to rise and

Choose a conifer suited to the moisture conditions in your garden. Bald-cypress thrives in wet, swampy sites.

radiate away from buildings and stone walls. Make sure your conifer selection is suited to both your macroclimate and the particular microclimate you have in mind.

SOIL

Conifers have an undeserved reputation for being very sensitive to soil type. While this is true to a certain extent for a few conifers (for example, most true firs are generally intolerant of poorly drained clay soils), beautiful conifers are available that will thrive in almost any soil. It is extraordinarily difficult to generalize about soil types throughout the country. The best way to determine the kind of soil in your garden is to submit samples to your Cooperative Extension office for analysis and then select conifers accordingly.

Soil pH is an especially important consideration when choosing conifers. Neutral soils have a pH from around 6 to 7, acid soils from 1 to 5 and basic or limy soils from 7 to 10. Some conifers — junipers, for example — perform better in relatively basic soils. Many southeastern pines, on the other hand, thrive in acid soils with pHs as low as 3.5 to 4.0.

MOISTURE

Moisture in the garden exists in many forms throughout the year: rain, fog, dew, relative humidity, snow, sleet, overhead and/or drip irrigation. The total annual precipitation in your area, the kinds (rain, snow, sleet) and the seasonal distribution (evenly throughout the year, for example, or only in one season) are all factors to consider when choosing conifers for your garden. Many tolerate periodic flooding in the winter, or quiescent season, but may be stressed or die if flooding occurs during the active growing season. Others, such as bald-cypress, thrive on permanently wet, swampy sites. The key is to choose conifers suited to the condi-

14

tions in your area and your garden. If, for example, you garden where there is an extended dry period in one season, it is best to use conifers such as some junipers and cypresses that will tolerate or even prefer such an extended dry period.

LIGHT

Light is essential to higher plants, but can also be a source of stress. Different plants are best adapted to different ranges of light intensity; some plants incur tissue damage when directly exposed to intense sunlight. Most garden books categorize the varying tolerances as "full sun," "partial shade" or "full shade." The gardener's challenge is to make sure plants receive enough light for growth without exposing them to overly intense light.

Some conifers, such as this Japanese cedar, will burn and bronze in the winter if planted in an overly exposed site.

Too much sun can be especially damaging in winter. A break of bright sunlight after weeks of dark, cloudy weather can result in both leaf and trunk sunscald. One way to avoid this problem, particularly if plants are borderline hardy for your area, is to wrap trunks of newly planted trees for the winter or to avoid siting plants where they get full southwesterly exposure.

Light intensity is key for variegated and colored selections. Some require intense light to develop full color, while others need protection to avoid leaf scorch.

AIR

Air is the source of oxygen for respiration and carbon dioxide for photosynthesis. It is also the source of potential pollutants, and the flow of air can create pockets or sustained blasts of excessive cold or heat. Winds near the coast can cause damage to salt-sensitive plants.

It's difficult to control air quality, but if it is a problem in your area you can
continues on page 18

SELECTING THE RIGHT PLANT FROM THE NURSERY: A CHECKLIST

The primary consideration when selecting plants for purchase is to choose the healthiest available individuals showing no signs of stress, pests or diseases.

SHOOTS

☐ The outer foliage should be free of browning or signs of insect damage. Some browning of interior foliage is common on dense, shrubby selections of junipers and spruces, as well as on many tight dwarf selections, and is not generally a problem.

☐ Resin accumulation on foliage and/or twigs is normal for some conifer species, either as small white specks or as accumulations of relatively clear or slightly cloudy gum. All twigs and branches, however, should be without heavy exudations or signs of insect boring and secondary fungal growth.

ROOTS

☐ If you're considering a container-grown conifer, ask your salesperson to slip a representative plant out of its container so you can check the root system. Avoid plants with circling roots or thick mats of roots, either at the soil surface or around the main stem. Look for the presence of clear white or cream-colored root tips near the soil surfaces (they may be yellow or even orange in some conifers), which indicate vigorous root growth.

☐ If you have the chance to inspect balled and burlapped (B&B) plants wrapped and ready to purchase from the lot, look for moist rootballs without large, torn, protruding primary root ends. Make sure that trunks and lower branches are free from any mechanical damage or girdling from the wrapping, and that rootballs are solid, and wider around than they are deep (more "tea cup"–shaped than perfectly spherical).

LARGE OR SMALL?

Is it better to purchase large plants for immediate impact or smaller ones that are less expensive and probably will better tolerate transplanting?

☐ Smaller is almost always better — with these exceptions:

☐ If you garden in an area subject to foot traffic, choose large rather than small, vulnerable plants.

☐ If you are planting very slow-growing dwarf forms and don't want to wait 20 years for an appropriate effect, buy a larger plant.

Most large conifers, such as this *Sciadopitys verticillata,* are best purchased balled and burlapped.

☐ If you have an immediate need for screening, plant rapidly growing selections that tolerate transplanting, using the smallest plants that will do the job.

CONTAINER OR BALLED & BURLAPPED?

In general, smaller, younger plants are available in containers, while larger, older material is available B&B or, in the western U.S., as boxed specimens. Most conifers perform admirably in either production system, with the following exceptions:

☐ Spruces are best purchased B&B,

as they are especially sensitive to root restriction.

☐ Species that form long tap roots, such as many pines, are best purchased B&B, although dwarf selections of the same pines will generally perform adequately in large containers.

GRAFTED OR OWN-ROOT

When chosen wisely, grafted plants can improve plant performance and diversify the garden palette. Many conifer cultivars, particularly those of pine, fir and most spruces, can only be propagated by grafting. Young shoots of conifers that can be successfully rooted as stem cuttings are often grafted onto a vigorous, more mature system for improved growth rate and development.

☐ When considering grafted plants, look for a cleanly healed graft wound with complete healing on all sides of the scion. Slight irregularities around the graft edges are normal, but there should be no obvious separation between scion, or grafted limb, and rootstock.

☐ Also, make sure that any remaining shoot growth from the understock is not overgrowing the shoot of the grafted selection — and that you can easily tell the difference so that you can trim away the understock shoot growth yourself without accidentally trimming away your cultivar shoot.

POLLUTANT-TOLERANT CONIFERS

The wax coating on the foliage of blue conifers offers some protection from air pollution. Blue cultivars of the following genera usually are good choices for polluted areas:

Abies (Fir)
Cedrus (Cedar)
Cunninghamia (China-Fir)
Cupressus (Cypress)
Picea (Spruce)
Pinus (Pine)
Sequoiadendron (Giant sequoia)
Sequoia (Redwood)

The following are generally pollution tolerant as well:

Juniperus (Juniper)
Larix (Larch)
Metasequoia (Dawn Redwood)
Pinus banksiana, P. cembra, P. contorta var. *latifolia, P. mugo, P. nigra, P. sylvestris, P. thunbergii*
Taxus cuspidata (Japanese Yew)
Thuja (Arborvitae)
Tsuga (Hemlock)
— *R. William Thomas*

Blue conifers, such as concolor fir, are relatively pollution-tolerant because their foliage is coated with wax.

choose a conifer that is relatively pollution tolerant (see "Pollution-tolerant Conifers," left). It is possible to modify air-flow patterns with buildings and wind breaks, or to select conifers that can stand up to strong prevailing winds.

PEST RESISTANCE

When selecting conifers, be sure to find out about diseases and pests that are problems in your region. If you're thinking of planting a Canadian hemlock in the eastern states, for example, you should know that it will require preventive treatment for hemlock woolly adelgid, probably for the lifetime of the plant. Your Cooperative Extension agent or local nursery professionals can advise you about pest- and disease-resistant selections.

Using Conifers in Your Garden

BY KIM TRIPP

ONIFERS AREN'T JUST stereotypical little green pyramids or looming forest trees. There is enough variation in shape, size, foliage color and texture, bark characteristics and ornamental cone types to whet any gardener's appetite. When looking for conifers to provide your garden with changing seasonal interest, consider the following ornamental qualities. For specific information on the characteristics of individual plants, see the Encyclopedia of Conifers on page 39.

COLOR

From the pink cones of the larch, to the blue foliage of the aptly named Colorado blue spruce, to the silver bark of the lacebark pine, the range of color in conifer cones, bark and foliage is vast. Emerald green arborvitae sprays, the coppery fall foliage of the dawn redwood and the plum-colored winter foliage of the Siberian juniper are just a few examples of extraordinary conifer coloration.

Both foliage and cones provide the primary color interest, with bark also playing a role. Cultivars of otherwise green species have been selected for distinctive blue or gold leaves and needles. Variegated selections also abound, some with showy splashes throughout the foliage, and others with subtle frostings on only the tips of the needles.

The foliage of many conifers changes color throughout the sea-

Conifers offer a spectrum of colors and textures from the soft, frosty blue foliage of the Boulevard false cypress (far left), to the feathery, brilliant bronze-gold of the deciduous larch in fall (left), to the rough bark of the Ponderosa pine that looks so inviting to touch (right).

sons. Some cultivars have been selected for contrasting new spring growth while others, like *Pinus strobus* 'Hillside Winter Gold', change color with the advent of cold weather and then return to a quieter green as the weather warms for the growing season. Deciduous conifers that develop fall colors before their needles drop — including shades of gold, bronze, bright yellow or cinnamon — add dimension to the range of foliage colors. The striking *Pseudolarix,* for example, turns a brilliant bronze-gold in the autumn months.

Seasonal changes in foliage color on evergreen plants are a function of temperature changes, while color change in fall foliage of deciduous conifers is analogous to that of other deciduous plants.

Cone colors offer still another range of ornamental possibilities. As cones develop, they may go through some very showy color stages, from bright violet in Korean firs to the shocking pink in true larches. These color changes are part of the cones' natural maturation processes.

A number of conifers have seeds or fleshy cones that look like brightly colored berries. For example, the red arils — the fleshy, berry-like covering on seeds of yews — sparkle among the foliage like crimson jewels.

Conifer barks can also be quite striking, with colors ranging from the cream-gray-green puzzle of young lacebark pine to the bright orange of mature Scots pine.

Ultimately, color is a personal and subjective choice. When selecting conifers for your garden, consider whether you want a riot of color or a more subdued color scheme with conifers of similar colors.

TEXTURE

Texture is a function of bark, foliage and the arrangement of branches. Evergreen selections offer a different kind of texture than deciduous conifers, whose foliage changes dramatically throughout the seasons — and even disappears altogether in winter to reveal the archi-
continues on page 23

CONIFERS FOR CONTAINERS

Conifers that you plan to plant in containers should be drought resistant and fully hardy — both the roots and the tops. Root hardiness is the key to successful container gardening with conifers. The roots of container-bound plants are exposed to much lower winter temperatures than roots in the ground. A good rule of thumb: if a plant is listed as hardy one or two USDA hardiness zones to your north, it is probably safe to grow in a container in your area.

Water stress is the other major challenge for container gardeners. Good drainage is essential, as is avoiding drought. Evergreens use water year round, and the soil in the container should never be allowed to completely dry out. This is as true in winter as in summer. Water whenever the soil is dry to the touch, anytime the soil is not frozen. Mulching not only helps reduce water stress but also helps insulate the soil from severe temperature swings.

Rot-resistant wood, such as cypress or teak, is the ideal material for containers. It has some insulating properties, doesn't dry out quickly and is not damaged by freezing and thawing. Pots made of plastic, fiberglass and other synthetic materials are resistant to cracking and don't dry out quickly. Concrete has both those advantages and is long lasting, attractive and paintable. Clay and terra cotta are not recommended for winter use in Canada and the northern half of the U.S. because they are easily cracked by freezing and thawing.

The following genera are some of the best choices for containers — especially the shrubby and dwarf plants, which look attractive alone or mixed with flowers and vines.

Juniperus (Juniper)
Chamaecyparis (False Cypress)
Pinus (Pine)
Tsuga (Hemlock)
Abies (Fir)
Picea (Spruce)

— *R. William Thomas*

The range of conifer "habits," or overall size and shape, includes everything from tiny dwarf bun selections to towering redwoods to magnificent pendulous forms like Sargent's weeping hemlock.

tecture and color of branches and trunk. The relatively broad, flattened needles of the Japanese umbrella pine offer bolder texture than the fine feathery needles of the eastern white pine, while the dark, platey bark of mature Japanese black pine has a vastly different texture from that of the lightly peeling, red-brown bark and deeply fluted trunk of dawn redwood.

The textural combinations you choose for your garden will reflect its unique style. Do you want a uniform sight-line of hedges down an allée or a more varied and natural-looking selection of textures? As with color, this is a matter of taste.

HABIT

Plant habit refers to both overall shape and size, as well as to the arrangement and display of branches along the trunk. For example, the overall outline of pendulous *Pinus strobus* 'Pendula' is that of a rounded pyramid with weeping branches. The narrowly columnar *Juniperus chinensis* 'Spartan' has the general outline of a broad pillar. Slow-growing and ground-hugging *Juniperus horizontalis* 'Mother Lode' is shaped like a dwarf pancake.

continues on page 25

DESIGNING WITH CONIFERS

Rather than relegating conifers to the nether regions of your garden, or plunking them smack in the middle of the lawn, enrich your plantings by treating them as versatile garden plants. Here are a few ideas:

Use conifers to give your garden an architectural framework. Because they retain their leaves year-round, evergreen conifers are ideal for defining spaces — framing vistas, creating rooms within a garden and forming backdrops for spring-blooming trees and shrubs. First consider placement and size: What space do you want defined and how do you want to define it? For partitioning off a kitchen garden or a perennial bed, use a low hedge such as a globe arborvitae. You can even use a low-growing conifer like a creeping juniper to define space next to a lawn.

Use conifers in utilitarian roles. Placed strategically, conifers can be used to block unsightly views, establish privacy, block wind or buffer loud noise. For example, if your intention is to block wind, you'll need to place a hedge running perpendicular to the direction of the prevailing wind. An 8'- to 15'-tall arborvitae makes an excellent windblock or garden wall. Tall, dense hedges can also muffle noise from traffic or schoolyards.

Mingle conifers with other plants. When choosing plants to combine with conifers, remember to consider color. Blue conifers look great with pink- and purple-flowering plants, yellow conifers set off yellow flowers and green conifers complement light-colored plants and flowers.

Use conifers as focal points. Shape is a particularly important consideration when using conifers as focal points or accent plants. Many gardeners, inspired by the grand columnar cypresses of Italy, try to re-create that effect at home. In California and the South, Italian cypresses do well. In colder northern regions, junipers or leyland cypresses make suitable substitutes. Enthusiastic gardeners are often taken with the shape of an unusual conifer such as a monkey puzzle tree. If you find yourself smitten by unusual specimens, be sure to limit your choice to just one or two types — overdo it with too many "focal points" and you won't know where to look first.

Don't just plant conifers in neat rows. If your garden is formal, space conifers at regular intervals. If not, note that even in Italy cypresses are often seen growing in masses or clusters as well as rows. For an informal look, stagger the spacing between the plants.   — *R. William Thomas*

You don't have to grow conifers in segregated conifer collections. This *Chamaecyparis pisifera* 'Filifera Aurea' is mingled with a variety of other plants in a striking flower border.

The habit of most coniferous trees changes over their lifetime. Younger plants tend to have more upright, conical habits that eventually spread and open with age. But this "rule" has so many exceptions that it is only a very general one at best.

The range of conifer shapes and sizes includes everything from tiny dwarf bun selections like the *Chamaecyparis obtusa* 'Elf', which after many decades of growth is still the the size of a softball, to the towering coastal redwoods of California — and everything in between. When choosing conifers for your garden, be sure to look beyond the formal conical habit so often associated with sheared Christmas trees and overused Colorado blue spruce.

MATURE SIZE

Every gardener wants to know how big a plant will grow and how fast it will get there. Homeowners want plants that will grow rapidly for a few years, reach some pre-determined size and shape and then remain static and unchanging until death. But that is not the way plants work. They reach a general size range at maturity that can be heavily influenced by the growing environment, but their ultimate size is only a guess.

In general, growth rates tend to be more rapid in young plants than in their older counterparts. Although there is some slowing with age, growth does not cease. Different plants do mature in different height classes and ranges (see "What is a Dwarf Conifer?," page 11), but growth rate and ultimate development is a function of many factors in addition to the plant's basic identity, including cli-

The easiest conifers to train as hedges are those, such as yew, that resprout on old wood.

CONIFERS FOR HEDGES

Almost any conifer can be trained as a hedge. The easiest ones to use are those that shear very well and resprout on old wood, such as plants in the following three genera:

Cephalotaxus (Plum Yew)

Taxus (Yew)

Thuja (Arborvitae)

Other conifers that tolerate shearing well but do not resprout on old wood include:

X *Cupressocyparis*

Cupressus (Cypress)

Juniperus (Juniper)

Podocarpus

Tsuga (Hemlock)

Pines, spruces and firs can be sheared in spring when the new growth has just emerged and is still soft, but not at any other time of the year. For this reason, they are much more difficult to maintain as hedges. If you don't mind the work, though, you can create a very unique hedge using these plants.

— *R. William Thomas*

mate, fertility, water availability, light intensity, propagation method and pruning practices.

What, exactly, do "mature height" or "ultimate size" mean? Plant height and spread at 5 years, 10 years, 50 years, 150 years? While the same plant grown in Minnesota and South Carolina may be perfectly hardy in both regions, it likely will exhibit very different growth rates in the warm Southeast than in the colder, northern Midwest. Entries in the Encyclopedia of Conifers, page 39, include estimates of average landscape size for plants grown in a reasonably non-stressful landscape environment; comments on regional variability and unusual growth rates are included where appropriate.

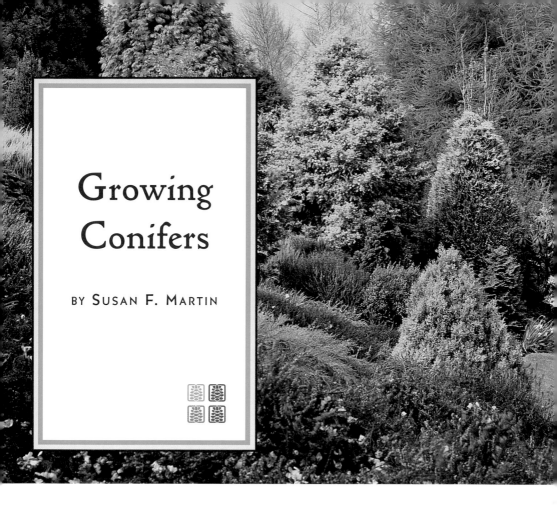

Growing Conifers

BY SUSAN F. MARTIN

One of the real bonuses of growing conifers is that they are so easy to maintain. The following guidelines will help even novice gardeners grow conifers successfully.

WHEN TO PLANT

Across most of the country, spring (early or late, depending on how far north you are) and early fall, when temperatures are cooler and rainfall more abundant, are the best times to plant conifers. To reduce transpiration or water loss from the tree, plant on an overcast day when there is ample soil moisture.

Avoid root-bound, container-grown plants that have a thick mat of roots or circling roots.

HOW TO PLANT

The hole you dig for your new conifer should be shallow and wide — twice the width of and more shallow than the height of the root ball. Unless the soil is very compacted or so light and porous that it retains very little moisture, you will not need to add organic matter. If soil drainage is a continual problem, consider creating a raised planting bed that has been amended to improve the soil.

When planting a conifer sold in a container, first loosen the roots by firmly tapping around the pot with the palm of your hand. Then, trim any roots that may be growing out of the drainage holes. If the plants are small, place your hand on the top of the pot, spreading your fingers so that the stem and the top of the soil are supported, and carefully slide the plant out, keeping the root ball intact. Tip large containers onto their sides to facilitate this process.

Many container-grown plants will have a mass of circling roots that should carefully be loosened by hand or with a small hand cultivator prior to planting. This will prevent the roots from girdling and eventually killing the plant.

Balled and burlapped (B&B) plants should be handled minimally and with care to prevent the root ball from breaking apart. B&B conifers are sometimes wrapped in plastic "burlap" or treated burlap, which may be green in color. These coverings do not decompose and should be removed before you fill in the hole with soil.

Plants in untreated burlap should be set into the prepared hole, which should then be filled about a third of the way with soil. Next, cut the burlap and cord away from the trunk and roll the burlap back to expose the top of the soil. Finally, you can fill in the rest of the hole, burying the burlap.

No matter how the plant was grown, be sure that the trunk flare (where the trunk and roots meet) is slightly higher than the surrounding soil level to compensate for settling, especially if your soil is heavy or poorly drained. Some root balls have soil above the trunk flare and it is best to remove it. Use excess soil to create a saucer or rim around the plant. This will allow water to collect, keeping the plant moist until it is established, and will provide extra soil when settling occurs. Always water thoroughly after planting.

Diligent care is critical from the time of planting until new roots are established. For the first few weeks, check the plant every two to three days for signs of stress and water whenever the soil feels dry. Once the roots

Unless the soil is very compacted or so light and porous that it retains little moisture, don't add organic matter when planting.

have grown out into the surrounding soil, which generally takes about three to six months, the plant can be checked less frequently.

WATERING

Established plantings need supplemental water only during periods of prolonged drought. The amount of water will depend on the species and your soil type. On average, water thoroughly if the top two to three inches of soil feel dry. Deep waterings when needed are better than frequent, shallow waterings. It's important to note that conifers do not show signs of stress as readily as other plants. For example, they seldom wilt; instead, the overall plant color will lighten or fade and interior needles will turn brown.

TO STAKE OR NOT TO STAKE

Conifers generally don't require staking, but there are three exceptions: Those used in very windy locations may need to be staked, but for no more than a year, long enough for anchor roots to develop sufficiently to support the plants. Staking is also beneficial for weeping or pendulous plants that are not yet self-supporting. Finally, if you want to espalier plants, they should be supported.

To prune a pine, pinch off half to two-thirds of the candle growth in spring. Candles are the shoots from which new needles emerge.

MULCHING

Mulching conifers is essential. It maintains the relatively cool soil temperatures that most conifers prefer. Mulching also helps conserve water and reduces weed competition. However, the mulch should be no more than two to three inches deep, and should never come in contact with the trunks of your plants.

FERTILIZING

Conifers are not heavy feeders and need only an annual application of a general, complete garden fertilizer such as 10-10-10 or 16-8-8, or a top dressing of well-rotted manure. It is best to fertilize in the early spring before the plants break dormancy, or in late fall before the soil freezes.

PRUNING

As with any plant, dead or diseased conifer branches should be removed immediately, regardless of the time of year. Any other pruning should be done when the plant is dormant. Unlike many deciduous shrubs, most conifers can't re-sprout from older wood (yew, arborvitae and podocarpus are exceptions), and so a good rule of thumb is never to remove more than one-third of the total growth at a time. If you prune too drastically, the plant may never fully recover. Many of the dwarf varieties never need to be pruned, but do appreciate some thinning to allow air and sunlight to penetrate to the interior of the plant.

The most common method of pruning evergreens is known as "cutting" or "heading" back. Only part of the branch is pruned; the terminal or tip growth is trimmed to side or lateral buds or branches. This promotes thicker, more compact foliage and a smaller overall plant.

Pines are pruned in a special way, called candling, to control growth. Candles are the elongated shoots from which the current season's needles will emerge. To prune a pine, remove one-half to two-thirds of the candle growth in the spring. Gently break the tips off by hand when the needles are just pushing out of the shoot. Do not use pruners as the blades will also cut the tips of the remaining needles, causing them to brown and discolor.

A type of mutation called a reversion is common in dwarf or variegated selections. A reversion is when these cultivars change back to the plant's "species form." Cultivars of some species, such as sawara false cypress, are especially prone to reversion. Familiarity with your particular cultivar will enable you to spot — and remove — a renegade branch quickly. To be sure that you have removed the area where the mutation originated, make the cut in the stable growth just below the point where the reversion has occurred.

Cultivars of some species such as Sawara false cypress, above, may revert back to the plant's "species form." Remove renegade branches as soon as you see them.

TRANSPLANTING

Sometimes a conifer will outgrow its location or you may decide that it really would look better on the other side of the yard. The most important factor when moving a conifer is the plant's size, which in turn determines the circumference of the root ball. Measure the trunk diameter about eight inches from the soil level. For each inch of diameter you should dig at least a foot in width of root ball. Consider hiring a professional to move any plant with a trunk diameter of much more than two inches.

Before digging, make sure that the soil is moist and the plant is in good health. Unhealthy specimens usually will not survive a transplant. Tie back branches so they are clear of the digging area. Then, mark the outline of the root ball in the soil as a guide. Begin by digging a trench around the outside of this guide line, clearing the soil from the hole. If you encounter large roots, cut them with pruning shears or loppers instead of the spade so that the roots do not tear and loosen the soil. Never walk or stand on top of the root ball while you are digging.

Mulching conifers is essential. It maintains the cool soil temperatures that most prefer.

The depth of the root ball will depend entirely on the depth of the roots of the plant. If the roots are fibrous and plentiful in the top 12 inches of soil, you will only need to dig a few inches deeper than that. If the roots appear to be sparse and random, you should dig deep enough to include as many roots as possible. Once the depth seems satisfactory, start to taper in towards the center of the hole. The final root ball should have a "tea cup" shape.

Next, wrap the ball tightly with burlap. Feed the end of a long strip of burlap around the ball and wrap spirally, beginning at the trunk and ending at the base. Leave enough burlap at the end to pull under the ball when the plant is moved. Secure the burlap edges with pinning nails, available from most horticultural suppliers.

Now, remove the ball from the hole. Using the digging spade, carefully under-cut the root ball and gently roll the plant enough to pull the loose section of burlap underneath the root ball. Secure the ends of the burlap tightly with nails.

To get the plant out of the hole, cut a six-foot length of burlap to make a cradle for the plant. Carefully tilt the plant to one side and work the middle of the strip of burlap under the root ball. Two people can now lift the conifer from the hole and carry it to the new site.

If possible, orient the transplanted conifer in the same direction as it was at the old site to prevent sun-scald that can occur when a shaded side of a conifer is suddenly exposed to full sun. The aftercare for transplanted conifers is exactly the same as that for newly planted specimens.

Thirteen Top Conifer Pests & Pathogens

BY R. WILLIAM THOMAS,
BRUCE STEWARD &
SCOTT AKER

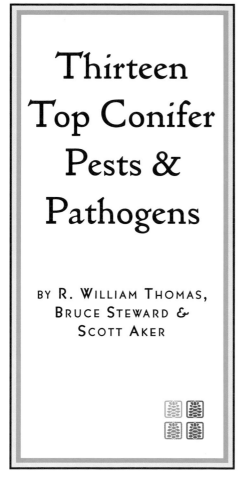

STRESS INCREASES A plant's susceptibility to pests. Planting too deeply, not allowing for adequate drainage, failure to mulch, over- or under-fertilizing and physical or winter injury are the most common causes of stress. You can often cure a pest or pathogen problem without the use of pesticides simply by alleviating the stress, and you can avoid potential problems by preventing stress in the first place.

Minor infestations often cause little harm and require no control. But they can indicate a major infestation in the offing. If you detect insects or indications of disease, first determine the severity of the problem. If you find only a few pests, identify them and continue to monitor the situation, checking to see whether their numbers are increasing. County Cooperative Extension offices, garden "hot lines" and reputable landscape pest-control companies are good resources both for identifying pests and keeping their populations under control. This chapter covers thirteen of the most serious pests and diseases of conifers, and the most sensible ways to control them.

I. SCALE INSECTS

Typically white, brown or gray, these sucking insects usually are visible on the leaves, stems and/or bark of conifers. While minor infestations may cause yellowing of the leaves, heavy infestations can severely weaken or kill the plant. To control scale, spray with horticultural oil or insecticidal soaps during summer, when the insects are most susceptible. Oils are relatively harmless to most non-target organisms but they can kill the immature stages of beneficial mites and insects; so be sure to time your spraying correctly so that repeat applications will not be necessary. During very hot, humid weather, avoid oil sprays on spruces altogether. To reduce chances of winter injury, avoid using oils on evergreens from late summer through mid-winter. Note: oil sprays will turn blue evergreens to green by dissolving the wax coating on their needles. New growth will again be blue.

2. MITES

To detect mites, tap a branch over a white piece of paper and look for light-colored, moving "dots," about the size of ground black pepper. These tiny pests suck juice from the needles, turning leaves gray to yellowish brown. Severe infestations will kill portions of the plant. Avoid planting mite-sensitive plants (see the  Encyclopedia of Conifers under specific species) in hot locations, especially where there is reflected light, heat and impeded air circulation due to walls and pavement. Use beneficial predatory mites, horticultural oil, plain water sprays or a variety of miticides (not general insecticides) to control an infestation.

3. BAGWORMS

These voracious caterpillars can quickly defoliate a plant. Because they carry their bag-like "houses" around with them, bagworms are most visible in summer, autumn and winter, when their bags are fairly large. An enlarged bag is about the size of a small pine cone. Remove the bags by hand; if done before late spring, this will prevent the eggs inside from hatching and attacking new growth. Insecticidal or bacterial (*Bacillus thuringiensis*) sprays aimed at the small caterpillars (usually in late spring/early summer) provide good control. For best control, spray when the bag is ¼" to ½" long.

4. HEMLOCK WOOLLY ADELGIDS

These sucking insects form globular, white waxy masses on twigs or needles of hemlocks, causing the needles to turn yellow and fall off. Control these pests

with horticultural oil in late spring, when the crawlers (the vulnerable immature insects) appear. From early summer through early October, follow-up sprays of horticultural oil or insecticidal soap may be warranted for controlling heavy infestations. Hemlock woolly adelgids are so prevalent in the Northeast that Canada hemlock is no longer recommended for planting there.

5. PINE BARK BEETLES

Serious and common pine pests, these beetles usually invade trees that are already weakened by pests or drought. However, they can attack healthy trees as well. The first indication of their presence is a sprinkling of sawdust pushed out of small holes by the adult beetles. Needles of affected branches turn yellow  and die. Because bark beetles are difficult to treat, prevention is the best method of control. Keep trees healthy by irrigating during extended droughts. Heavily infested, dying trees should be destroyed (burned or buried) to prevent adult beetle emergence.

6. TIP MOTH

 These small caterpillars can be very destructive to two- and three-needled pines like lodgepole or Monterey pine. In severe cases, they will kill nearly all of the tip growth. (Five-needled pines are not affected by pine tip moths but sustain similar damage inflicted by the white pine weevil.) The damage from either insect is disfiguring but does not usually kill the tree. Look for small, brown pupae, slightly larger than a grain of rice, inside the dead tips to confirm tip moth damage. Control with pesticides is difficult because inside the tip growth, the caterpillars remain immune from their effects. You can eliminate tip moths by breaking off the damaged tips and destroying the pupae inside. Bacterial (*Bacillus thuringiensis*) sprays are effective if applied just after the caterpillars emerge and before they tunnel into the shoot. Check plants three times a week for the recently hatched caterpillars in spring and summer. Be sure to take advantage of this opportunity to spray with the nontoxic *Bt.*

PINE NEEDLE DROP

Every autumn, as the interior needles on their pines turn tannish brown and drop, worried gardeners and homeowners call horticultural hot lines in a panic. All pines experience needle drop in autumn. The easiest way to determine if this is natural or the result of a pest is by inspecting a branch. If the needles at the end of the branch are green and healthy looking, the plant is healthy. If, however, the end needles are dying, there is a pest or other serious problem.

7. DEER

While electrified fences, mesh coverings over plants, sprays and dogs can all reduce damage by browsing deer, there are no foolproof deterrents — particularly if their population grows large enough. A number of plants have been touted as "deer-proof" or "deer-resistant." However, hungry deer will eat just about anything; "deer-resistant" plants simply become their second choice. Deer preferences vary regionally. For example, eastern arborvitae, a native of eastern North America, is a favorite of Eastern deer but is generally ignored by Western deer, who prefer western arborvitae. In the East, western arborvitae is considered "deer-resistant."

8. DIPLODIA TIP BLIGHT

This fungal disease affects two- and three-needled pines such as mugho or Scots pine, causing branch dieback. A severe case will eventually kill the tree. If you detect evidence of tip blight on susceptible pines, spray new growth with protective fungicidal sprays in spring. Spray after the candles are fully extended, but before the needles are exposed. Two weeks later, spray again, and two weeks after that, apply a third application. Remove dead branches during dry weather in late fall. Discard or burn any fallen needles or cones.

9. CYTOSPORA CANKER

This fungus attacks spruces and Italian cypress, usually killing lower branches first. Plant injury, such as that incurred by lawn mowers and breakage due to ice and snow, allows entry of spores. There is no recommended fungicidal control for this disease. Removal and disposal of dead branches during dry weather and watering during drought conditions can help to keep it under control.

10. CORYNEUM CANKER

This fungus attacks cypresses — especially Monterey, Italian and Leyland cypress. Symptoms and treatment are the same as for cytospora canker.

11. PHOMOPSIS TIP BLIGHT

This fungal disease causes the tips of juniper branches to turn brown, and sometimes results in the death of the entire branch. The fruiting bodies of the fungus — the structures that release the spores by which the disease is spread — appear as small, black dots on recently killed leaves. The disease is most severe in hot, humid weather and when plants are growing in locations with poor air circulation. Control tip blight by pruning and destroying infected twigs and branches. Several sprays of a fungicide at two-week intervals beginning in early spring may help.

12. KABATINA TWIG BLIGHT

Fairly common on some of the creeping junipers, including 'Andorra' and 'Blue Chip', especially in parts of the Midwest, this fungal disease damages and kills year-old twigs. It enters the plant through wounds caused by insects, winter damage or pruning, usually becoming evident before new growth starts in the spring. Prevention of injury is the best control.

13. CEDAR RUST

Cedar rust completes part of its life-cycle on susceptible junipers (sometimes called cedars) and the other part on a nearby apple, hawthorn, quince or serviceberry. The symptoms appear on junipers as brown, corky galls up to two inches in diameter. The galls appear in autumn and last through the winter. In spring, they produce orange "horns" that release spores that then attack the alternate host plant (apple, etc.). Chief injury is to the alternate host, with the juniper sustaining minor damage. Avoid planting susceptible junipers (eastern red cedar is the most likely to have problems) near susceptible apples, crabapples and hawthorns. Galls can be removed by hand. Applying fungicidal sprays in mid- to late summer can prevent infection.

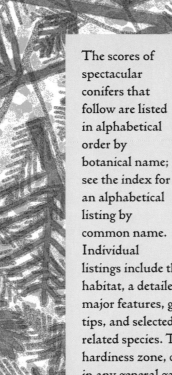

Encyclopedia of Conifers

The scores of spectacular conifers that follow are listed in alphabetical order by botanical name; see the index for an alphabetical listing by common name. Individual listings include the plant's native habitat, a detailed description of its major features, growing and design tips, and selected cultivars and related species. To find your hardiness zone, check the zone map in any general garden reference or the detailed maps in the **Sunset Western Garden Book**, published by the editors of Sunset books and **Sunset** magazine.

CONCOLOR OR WHITE FIR

Abies concolor

NATIVE HABITAT

Colorado to Baja California

HARDINESS ZONES

USDA 4-7, Sunset 1-9, 14-24

DESCRIPTION

A dense, pyramidal tree, 50' tall by 20' wide. Grows up to 12" per year. The flat, bluish green needles are curved, soft, waxy and up to 3" in length. Cones are upright, and disintegrate when ripe.

GARDEN USE

A good specimen tree, especially where blue color is useful. Very similar to Colorado spruce, but much softer in effect. Makes an unusual hedge plant when new growth is sheared.

HOW TO GROW

Needs full sun and well-drained soil. Scale insects and balsam woolly adelgid are occasionally problems; otherwise, concolor fir is quite healthy in its range. Unlike many firs, it is tolerant of hot summers and thus useful in many areas of the country.

CULTIVARS AND RELATED SPECIES

'Candicans' — A standard-size tree with long, silvery blue needles. Other blue-leaved trees include forma *argentea*, 'Glenmore' and 'Violacea'.

'Compacta' — An irregularly shaped shrub with blue needles.

'Conica' — A compact, pyramidal shrub.

A. grandis, Grand Fir — A western species that is useful in much of the West, but unsuccessful in the East. Grows 60' tall in gardens (300' in the wild), with dark-green needles to 2" long, white underneath. USDA Zone 6, Sunset 1-9, 14-17.

A. lasiocarpa 'Compacta', Compact Alpine Fir — A dwarf, bright blue, conical plant. Grows about 3"-6" in height per year. USDA Zones 5-7, Sunset 1-9, 14-17.

A. procera 'Glauca', Blue Noble Fir — A large tree with silvery blue needles. USDA Zones 6-7, Sunset 1-7, 15-17.

FRASER FIR

NATIVE HABITAT

Mountains of West Virginia, North Carolina and Tennessee

HARDINESS ZONES

USDA 4-6, Sunset 3-7, 15-17

DESCRIPTION

A pyramidal tree to 40' tall and 20' wide, with stiff, horizontal branches. Grows 8"-12" per year. Needles are flat, dark green, ½"-1" long, whitish underneath and borne radially on the upper side of the branch. Cones are purple and upright, and disintegrate when ripe. One of the most popular cut Christmas trees. Also popular as a "living" Christmas tree, but generally these do not thrive once they are planted in the garden. It and *A. balsamea* are often used as rootstocks for other firs.

GARDEN USE

Beautiful as a specimen or in a grouping.

HOW TO GROW

Needs full sun, ample moisture and relatively cool summers. Unhealthy and short-lived in regions with hot, dry weather.

CULTIVARS AND RELATED SPECIES:

'Prostrata' — A mounding dwarf, eventually reaching 4'-5' high and 12' wide.
A. balsamea, Balsam Fir — A pyramidal tree with V-shaped sprays of fragrant needles. It reaches about 60' high, 20' wide. Useful only in northern and mountainous zones. USDA Zones 2-5, Sunset 3-7, 15-17.
A. balsamea 'Nana' — A popular small shrub that grows less than 3" per year. Forma *hudsonia* is very similar.

Abies fraseri

NORDMANN FIR

NATIVE HABITAT
Caucasus Mountains of Eurasia

HARDINESS ZONES
USDA 5-7, Sunset 1-11, 14-24

DESCRIPTION
A pyramidal tree, 50' tall by 20' wide. Grows up to 12" per year. Branches droop, so the tree always seems fully clothed at the base. Flat, dark green, 1" long, fragrant needles are silver underneath. Cones are upright, disintegrating when ripe.

Abies nordmanniana

HOW TO GROW
Needs full sun and well-drained soil. Scale insects occasionally are a problem. One of the best firs for areas with hot summers. Received the Pennsylvania Horticultural Society's Gold Medal in 1994.

A. nordmanniana, foliage

GARDEN USE
A beautifully dense, dark-green specimen tree. Needles look as if they have been brushed forward. The undersides of the needles give occasional glimpses of silver.

CULTIVARS AND RELATED SPECIES
A. firma, Momi Fir — One of the most heat-tolerant firs. Grows to 70' tall by 30' wide. USDA Zones 6-7 (perhaps warmer), Sunset 5-11, 14-24.
A. koreana, Korean Fir — A relatively small tree, rarely growing over 35' tall, with dark-green needles. Cones are purple and can be very attractive. USDA Zones 5-7, Sunset 1-11, 14-24.
A. pinsapo, Spanish Fir — A beautiful narrow fir 60' tall by 15' wide, with rigid, green needles. USDA Zones 6 to 7, Sunset 5-11, 14-24.

MONKEY PUZZLE TREE, CHILE PINE

NATIVE HABITAT
Andes of south-central Chile and Argentina

HARDINESS ZONES
USDA 7b-10, Sunset 4-9, 14-24

DESCRIPTION
A large evergreen tree to over 100' tall in the wild, generally 20'-40' in gardens with half the spread. Grows 6"-12" per year. Horizontal, whorled branches. Open, round-headed habit with age. Unusual flat, dark-green, sharp-pointed leaves 1"-2" long, arranged spirally around the branches. Cones are heavy and 5"-8" long on older female plants. The large cones can be very dangerous when they fall.

GARDEN USE
The bold effect created by this plant's habit and foliage make it a remarkable specimen. There are many venerable and extraordinary specimens of monkey puzzle tree in old gardens around the world.

HOW TO GROW
Plant in full sun in well-drained, moist locations. Provide even moisture, especially during the first two full growing seasons. Moderately

Araucaria araucana

tolerant of salt spray in coastal areas.

CULTIVARS AND RELATED SPECIES
Cultivars of *A. araucana* are rare in the U.S.
A. heterophylla, Norfolk Island Pine — Grown as a house plant and indoor Christmas tree, and outdoors in Florida and southern California. USDA Zone 10, Sunset 17, 21-24.

A. araucana, foliage

INCENSE CEDAR, PENCIL CEDAR

NATIVE HABITAT
California, Baja California and adjacent Mexico, southwestern Nevada, Oregon

HARDINESS ZONES
USDA 6(5b)-10, Sunset 1-12, 14-24

DESCRIPTION
A large evergreen tree to over 150' in the wild, usually to 40'-80' in cultivation, with a very narrow spread. Upright, flattened sprays of bright-green foliage. Small, tan, erect cones. The tree's oil has an incense-like odor.

GARDEN USE
Its narrowly pyramidal to conical habit with no shearing, relatively rapid growth rate and exceptionally good winter color make this a choice evergreen for hedges and screens. Will tolerate light shade without losing density of foliage cover. The red-brown bark of this tree is very ornamental.

HOW TO GROW
Plant in full sun or light shade in a range of soils. Provide even moisture for the first two full growing seasons. Protect variegated cultivars from high winds and intense winter sun to avoid burning. Native populations of this plant range from low elevation forests to over 6,000' in the Sierra Nevada, with resulting variation in cold tolerance. If you garden in USDA Zones 8 or colder be sure to acquire plants propagated from stock native to high-elevation areas.

CULTIVARS AND RELATED SPECIES:
'Aureovariegata' — Has foliage liberally splashed with creamy yellow. 'Berrima Gold' and 'Maupin Glow' — Two recently introduced uniformly yellow-gold selections. 'Compacta' — A rounded, slower-growing form with gray-green foliage.

Calocedrus decurrens

ATLAS CEDAR

NATIVE HABITAT

Atlas Mountains of northern Africa

HARDINESS ZONES

USDA 6-10, Sunset 4-23

DESCRIPTION

An evergreen tree that can become 60' tall by 50' wide at maturity. Grows 6"-12" per year. Needles are ¾"-1" long, bluish green, in whorls on short spur shoots. Cones are oval, 3" long by 2"-2½" wide, and disintegrate upon ripening. Habit is open and pyramidal when young, wide-spreading and picturesque with age.

GARDEN USE

A spectacular specimen plant for the large-scale garden or landscape, although many cultivars offer unusual or dwarf habits that would be adaptable to any garden. The glaucous selections are silvery blue and make wonderful accent plants.

HOW TO GROW

Performs best in full sun and well-drained soils. Needs to be protected from winter winds. Spider mites and scale are occasional problems.

continues on page 46

Cedrus atlantica 'Glauca'

CULTIVARS AND RELATED SPECIES

'Glauca', Blue Atlas Cedar — Needles conspicuously bluish. Same size as other trees of the species. Tolerates air pollution.

Cedrus libani

'Glauca Pendula', Weeping Blue Atlas Cedar — Branches droop vertically. Very dramatic and easily trained as a specimen or espalier.

C. libani, Cedar of Lebanon — Similar in appearance to *C. atlantica,* with thinner, longer and darker green needles.

Note: Some publications now list *C. atlantica* as a subspecies of *C. libani,* and its name appears as *Cedrus libani* ssp. *atlantica.* Because cultivars of both plants may have the same cultivar name (for example, 'Pendula'), *C. atlantica* cultivars that share a name with a *C. libani* selection are now listed with 'Atlantica' in their names — for example, *C. libani* 'Atlantica Pendula'.

C. libani 'Green Prince' — A dark green, dwarf shrub with an irregular growth habit. Resembles a miniature bonsai.

C. libani var. *stenocoma* — The most cold hardy *C. libani*, with a stiff, pyramidal habit.

C. deodara, Deodar Cedar — The least cold hardy of the true cedars, with 1"-2", bluish-green needles. Mature plants broaden with age and become flat-topped.

C. deodara 'Aurea' — A selection with yellow foliage. Very beautiful in the spring when the new growth flushes out.

C. deodara 'Snow Sprite' — A dwarf selection with a mounding habit. All of the new growth flushes white. Winter burn in exposed sites may be a problem.

JAPANESE PLUM YEW

NATIVE HABITAT
Japan and parts of China and Korea

HARDINESS ZONES
USDA 6(5b)-10, Sunset 4-9, 14-17

DESCRIPTION
An evergreen shrub very similar in appearance to true yew (*Taxus*). Informal spreading habit from prostrate to upright and shrubby, reaching 2'-8' tall with spreads of 4'-12', depending on the selection. Coarse, dark green needles are whitish underneath. Seeds with fleshy, reddish outer coats resemble small plums at maturity on female plants.

GARDEN USE
Slow to moderate growth rate and graceful informal habit. Good low to medium ground cover or screen, especially across areas with a range of light conditions or soil types. Excellent evergreen for shaded sites and for combining in a mixed border or small garden.

HOW TO GROW
Plant in full sun or shade in a range of soils, from well drained to wet, heavy clay. Provide even moisture for the first two full growing seasons. Much more heat tolerant than true yew and generally unappealing to deer. Can be sheared in moderation.

CULTIVARS AND RELATED SPECIES
'Duke Gardens' — A compact, shrubby form.
'Fastigiata' — Habit is upright and columnar in young plants but eventually becomes rounded and spreading.
'Korean Gold' — New foliage emerges bright yellow-gold in the spring and gradually fades to green.
'Prostrata' — A low and spreading form with a cloud-like silhouette. Winner of the Pennsylvania Horticultural Society's Gold Medal.
C. fortunei — Not as hardy (USDA Zones 6b-10), but has elegant, very long needles.
C. koreana — A Korean species typically even more cold hardy than *C. harringtonia*.

Cephalotaxus harringtonia

ALASKA-CEDAR

NATIVE HABITAT
Northern California to Alaska

HARDINESS ZONES
USDA 5-7, Sunset 4-6, 15-17

DESCRIPTION
An evergreen tree that reaches 100' or more in the wild, 60' in gardens, with a pyramidal habit. Grows 8"-12" per year. Leaves are scale-like, without white marks on the undersides. Branchlets are pendulous and arranged in a vertical plane, especially near the top of the tree. Cones are round with 4-6 scales.

GARDEN USE
Use as a single specimen or in a broad hedge row. Thrives best in moist soils. There are several cultivars, including the magnificent 'Pendula', which is quite picturesque.

HOW TO GROW
Prefers full sun, humidity and moist, cool soil to thrive. Very durable and tolerant of many soil types as long as there is ample moisture.

CULTIVARS:
'Compacta' — A dwarf shrub with a rounded habit. Eventually becomes 6' in height and equally as wide.
'Green Arrow' — Tall and strictly narrow, with vertically weeping branches.
'Pendula' — A broadly pyramidal selection with drooping branchlets.

Chamaecyparis nootkatensis

HINOKI FALSE CYPRESS

NATIVE HABITAT
Japan and Taiwan

HARDINESS ZONES
USDA 5-8, Sunset 4-6, 15-17

DESCRIPTION
At maturity, a narrow tree with a rounded crown to 40' in cultivation. Grows 8"-12" per year. Leaves are scale-like and dark green, with glaucous banding below. Cones are woody and round, ⅓"- ½" in diameter. Bark is reddish brown, deeply furrowed and peels with age.

GARDEN USE
Outstanding for its dense, dark green foliage, shade tolerance and durability. The species can be used as a hedge or screen, in containers or as a replacement for Canada hemlock. Dwarf cultivars from 12" to 12' can be used in trough and rock gardens and perennial and shrub borders, or as specimens.

HOW TO GROW
Grows best in moist, well-drained soil in full sun or light shade. Very root hardy, it grows well in containers. Performs poorly in much of the Midwest.

CULTIVARS:
'Crippsii' — A pyramidal selection to 30'. Foliage is golden yellow. Plant in full sun for best color.
'Nana Gracilis' — Perhaps the best known cultivar. Broadly conical in habit, with dark green, cupped foliage. Grows slowly to 5' in 20 years. 'Nana' and 'Nana Gracilis' often are catch-all names for any dwarf selection of unknown identity.
'Split Rock' — A dwarf, rounded shrub with blue, needle-like juvenile foliage.

Chamaecyparis obtusa 'Crippsii'

'Tetragona Aurea' — A dwarf, upright selection with branches arranged irregularly. Branchlets are four-sided. Needles are glossy and golden, and in four rows. May reach 12'-15' tall at 30 years.

SAWARA FALSE CYPRESS

NATIVE HABITAT
Japan

HARDINESS ZONE
USDA 4-8, Sunset 4-6, 15-17

DESCRIPTION
A tree to 60' with a pyramidal form. Grows 8"-12" per year. Leaves are generally medium green and scale-like with glaucous banding beneath. The tips of the scales are pointed. Cones are small and rounded, to ¼" in diameter. As the plants age, the cinnamon-colored bark peels.

GARDEN USE
This variable species has many out-standing cultivars. The species is beautiful in mass plantings. Cultivars vary in habit and can be grown as specimens or in a border. Some are easily sheared and thus useful as hedging and topiaries. Roots are hardy, making this cypress good for containers (Zones 6-8).

HOW TO GROW
Prefers a moist, well-drained soil and full sun to partial shade. Also benefits from an annual removal of debris and dead foliage from interior branches. Many cultivars produce "reversions," or branches that have mutated back to the "species form" of the plant. Such reversions should be removed by pruning.

CULTIVARS AND RELATED SPECIES
'Boulevard' — An upright, pyramidal tree with awl-shaped needles that curve inward. Silvery blue color in summer, more grayish in winter. 'Filifera Aurea' — Golden yellow, thread-like, nodding branches. Becomes a broad, conical specimen to 15' in height in 30 years. Smaller, golden versions of thread-leaf cypress include 'Golden Mop' and 'Golden Pincushion'. They are more cold hardy than the species.

Chamaecyparis pisifera

ATLANTIC WHITE CEDAR

NATIVE HABITAT

Maine, south to Florida, in coastal plain swamps and bogs

HARDINESS ZONES

USDA 4-9, Sunset 4-6, 15-17

DESCRIPTION

Scale-like leaves have sharply pointed tips. Needles have white margins and oil glands. Cones are rounded, ¼" in diameter, with 4-5 scales, and are usually quite numerous. An upright tree to 50', with a narrowly columnar habit. Grows 8"-12" per year. Often found growing on wet sites in its native habitat.

GARDEN USE

Its narrow habit makes this useful as a hedge or screen, or in a mass planting. Several dwarf selections make fine rock-garden plants, provided there is ample soil moisture.

HOW TO GROW

A fine choice for planting in a low or wet area of the garden. Prefers full sun. Will grow in average soils, but is not drought tolerant.

CULTIVARS AND RELATED SPECIES

'Andelyensis' — A narrowly columnar form to 10'. Foliage is an attractive gray-green, with a mixture of adult and juvenile needles. Cones are usually abundant. Not as cold hardy as the species.

'Heatherbun' — Flat-topped and globe-shaped in habit, this dwarf selection has juvenile needles that turn plum-colored in the winter months.

'Little Jamie' — A dwarf, densely compact, narrow column. Leaves are small, fine-textured and blue-green.

Chamaecyparis thyoides

JAPANESE CEDAR

NATIVE HABITAT
Japan and parts of China and Korea

HARDINESS ZONES
USDA 6b-10, Sunset 4-9, 14-24

DESCRIPTION
A large evergreen tree to over 100' in the wild, usually seen at heights of 30'-70' in cultivation with half the spread. Grows rapidly. Numerous dwarf and slow-growing cultivars are available. Habit is informally pyramidal to conical. Small, awl-shaped, medium-green needles are arranged in whorls around narrow branchlets. Cones are small, tan, round, about 1" in diameter and scattered throughout the foliage.

Cryptomeria japonica, foliage

GARDEN USE
Tolerant of a wide range of soils from sands to moderately heavy clays. The relatively narrow profile with good foliage cover and fine-textured needles creates a soft, informal appearance for a large conifer. Unusual tolerance of poorly drained clay soils (but not perennially flooded sites) and hot climates makes it especially good in the humid Southeast. Unfortunately, tends to brown in Mid-Atlantic winters. *Cryptomeria* is a small genus of one species, but many cultivars of Japanese cedar have been selected over the centuries both in Asia and Europe. Cultivars range from extreme dwarfs to fast-growing selections appropriate for screening. Old seedling trees in decline can be found in many established gardens but these plants are not representative of the excellent landscape quality and performance provided by the many good cultivars now available.

HOW TO GROW

Plant in full sun (light shade for dwarf and year-round variegated selections) in a range of soils. Provide even moisture for the first three full growing seasons. Tolerant of moderate drought once established. Avoid extremely exposed and windy sites in northern gardens to prevent excessive winter bronzing and burning.

CULTIVARS AND RELATED SPECIES

'Benjamin Franklin' — Grows as tall as the species, with good wind tolerance and some tolerance of salt spray.

'Elegans' — A large, often multi-stemmed plant with soft, needle-like leaves that turn a plum color in winter.

'Elegans Nana' — A low shrub that is otherwise similar to 'Elegans'.

'Globosa Nana' — A rounded and bushy cultivar.

'Little Diamond' — A dense bush similar to, but smaller than 'Globosa Nana'; does very well in the Southeast.

'Rasen' — A selection with thin shoots and twisted leaves. Thrives in the Southeast.

'Rein's Dense Jade' — A dense, mounding shrub with dark green foliage. Heat-tolerant.

'Sekkan-sugi' — A tall cultivar with cream to light yellow new spring growth.

'Tenzan Yatsubusa' — An extreme dwarf.

'Yoshino' — A tree cultivar that is probably the most cold hardy in the U.S. Has a uniformly narrow form and maintains a good green color throughout the year. Recipient of the Pennsylvania Horticultural Society's Gold Medal.

C. japonica

CHINA-FIR

NATIVE HABITAT
Central and southern China

HARDINESS ZONES
USDA 6-8, Sunset 4-6, 14-21

DESCRIPTION
A broadly pyramidal tree with strongly horizontal branches, 75' tall by 30' wide. Grows up to 12" per year. Needles are stiff, bluish green, pointed, prickly, to 2½" long, with two white bands beneath. Buds in tufts at tips of branches. Cones are oval, 2" long by 1½" wide.

GARDEN USE
An interesting tree with a unique texture and very attractive reddish orange bark. Tolerates shade, heat and heavy clay soils better than many conifers and is thus useful in the Southeast. Rare in the North but widely used in the South and occasionally on the Pacific Coast.

HOW TO GROW
Plant in sun or partial shade. Protect from winter winds in northern part of its range. Generally needs no pruning although, if pruned severely, the tree has the unusual ability to resprout. Mites are occasionally a problem. Plants grown from cuttings may need training to form a central leader. *Cunninghamia* tends to be messy, because it holds old, dead foliage, which detracts from its ornamental value.

CULTIVARS AND RELATED SPECIES
'Chason's Gift' — A uniformly pyramidal form that is dark green in color.
'Glauca' — Blue foliage. More attractive and hardier than other plants of the species. May turn purplish in winter if in full sun.
C. konishii, Formosan Cunninghamia — Very similar to the above species, but is less hardy, with smaller leaves (1" long) and cones. Some botanists believe it is not actually a different species.

Cunninghamia lanceolata 'Glauca'

LEYLAND CYPRESS

NATIVE HABITAT

Hybrid between *Cupressus macrocarpa* (Monterey Cypress) and *Chamaecyparis nootkatensis* (Alaska-cedar), both native to western North America.

HARDINESS ZONES

USDA 6-8, Sunset 3-24

DESCRIPTION

A tall, narrowly columnar tree reaching heights of 80'-100'. Leaves are scale-like and generally dark green to gray-green, in flattened sprays. Branches are 4-sided or cylindrical. Although scarce, cones are round, to ¾" in diameter.

GARDEN USE

Most often used as a screen plant because of its rapid growth rate — up to 3' per year. Also lovely when grown as a hedge, or as a single specimen allowed to reach its fullest potential. Several pests and diseases are now associated with Leyland cypress, so it is best planted in conjunction with other plants rather than as a monotypic hedge. Unfortunately, it is becoming over-planted. Farmed as a Christmas tree in the southern states.

HOW TO GROW

Prefers a sunny location protected from strong winds. Tends to have a weak root system and is best planted in the spring. Larger plants do not transplant well. Bagworms, spider mites and stem canker diseases are occasionally a problem. Tolerates shearing well, but does not resprout from old wood.

CULTIVARS AND RELATED SPECIES

'Castlewellan' — A golden selection.
'Leighton Green' — The clone that is most commonly sold in the trade. Maintains dark green coloration in all seasons.
'Naylor's Blue' — Blue-green foliage.
'Silver Dust' — Foliage has creamy variegation throughout.

X Cupressocyparis leylandii

ARIZONA SMOOTH CYPRESS

NATIVE HABITAT

Central Arizona

HARDINESS ZONES

USDA 7-9, Sunset 5, 8-24

DESCRIPTION

A pyramidal to columnar tree, usually under 60' tall in garden settings. Scale-like, overlapping leaves are arranged in four rows. Tip of the leaf is sharply pointed. Branchlets are held at roughly 90° to the main branch. Foliage color varies from blue-green to gray-green. Cones are round, and 1"-1¼" in diameter. Bark is smooth and mahogany colored.

GARDEN USE

Use as a specimen, in a mass planting or as a hedgerow plant.

Cupressus macrocarpa

HOW TO GROW

Like all cypresses, thrives in hot sun and well-drained soils. Very drought tolerant.

CULTIVARS AND RELATED SPECIES

'Blue Ice' — A narrow, columnar tree with baby-blue foliage. Is also listed as *C. glabra* 'Blue Ice'.
'Carolina Sapphire' — Another selection with intense blue foliage. Introduced from South Carolina.
C. cashmeriana, Kashmir Cypress — Native to the Himalayas. A choice species valued for its long, pendulous, flattened branches and pyramidal habit. Hardy to perhaps USDA Zone 9.
C. macrocarpa, Monterey Cypress — Endemic to California's Monterey Peninsula. A pyramidal tree with bright green foliage. Prefers cool, breezy coastal sites, and does not tolerate the high heat and humidity of the Southeast. Numerous cultivars with varying foliage colors are available. USDA Zones 7-9, Sunset 17.
C. sempervirens, Italian Cypress — A slender tree to 60' with dense, dark green foliage. USDA Zones 7-9, Sunset 8-15,18-20.
C. sempervirens 'Swane's Golden' —

C. sempervirens 'Swane's Golden'

Bears golden yellow foliage and is quite beautiful in the warmer zones where it can be grown.
C. sempervirens 'Stricta' — Easily identified by its very narrow, formal appearance and gray-green leaves. Commonly grown in California.

CHINESE JUNIPER

NATIVE HABITAT
China, Japan and Korea

HARDINESS ZONES
USDA 3-9, Sunset 1-16, 18-21

DESCRIPTION
The species, in nature an evergreen shrub or tree to over 50' with a broad crown, is rarely seen in cultivation, but the plethora of cultivars includes every habit imaginable. Foliage is generally blue- or gray-green and of two types: small, scale-like leaves tightly pressed to the stem (called "adult") and needle-like foliage in whorls around the stem (called "juvenile").

GARDEN USE
The huge diversity of cultivars makes generalizations about habit and garden use impossible. Most selections are tough, reliable garden plants in full sun.

HOW TO GROW
Plant in full sun (only!) and well-drained soils. Provide even moisture for the first full growing season.

CULTIVARS AND RELATED SPECIES
'Kaizuka' (or 'Torulosa'), Hollywood Juniper — A very popular contorted, small tree or large shrub.
'Pfitzeriana', Pfitzer Juniper — A large, spreading shrub.
'Robusta Green' — Has an upright, irregular habit and dense blue-green foliage.
'San Jose' — A popular, low-spreading ground cover.
'Saybrook Gold' — Has striking gold foliage.
'Spartan' — A tall, remarkably columnar plant.
J. davurica, Dahurian Juniper, and *J. sabina*, Savin Juniper — Two related, useful garden species with cultivars that are superior to the parent species.
J. davurica 'Expansa Variegata' — A widely available cream-variegated selection with a low, spreading habit.
J. davurica 'Parsoni', Parsons Juniper — A good choice for hot southern gardens.

Juniperus chinensis 'Kaizuka'

COMMON JUNIPER

NATIVE HABITAT

Much of the Northern Hemisphere

HARDINESS ZONES

USDA 2-7, Sunset 1-12, 18-20

DESCRIPTION

Evergreen, multistemmed shrub to tree reaching 40' in some areas. Great variation in form and habit among both wild populations and cultivars. Needle-like foliage, arranged in whorls, has a conspicuous white band.

GARDEN USE

Generally quite cold hardy and stress tolerant, particularly of dry, poor, rocky soils but less tolerant of climates where heat is accompanied by high humidity and heavy rainfall (for example, the Southeast). Bark on older plants can develop handsome, red-brown color with some exfoliation. An excellent species for tough, dry, sunny sites in northern climates. Unusually prominent, white bands on needles are especially attractive.

HOW TO GROW

Plant in full sun in well-drained soil. Provide even moisture for the first full growing season.

continues on page 60

Juniperus communis

CULTIVARS AND RELATED SPECIES

'Berkshire' — Develops into a broad cushion with a much denser habit than the species and shorter, blue-hued needles.

'Compressa' — A very tight dwarf column that is seen in many rock gardens and is somewhat less cold hardy than the species.

'Depressa' — Actually a group of clonally propagated selections of the botanical variety *depressa* (old-field juniper) with a somewhat upright, broad-spreading habit. Both the trade stand-by 'Depressa' (more correctly known as 'Depressed Star') and 'Depressa Aurea' with bright gold upper foliage are very satisfactory performers.

'Hornibrookii' — A low-growing, semi-prostrate shrub with unique tight foliage that appears braided.

J. rigida, Needle Juniper— Generally a small tree 15'-20' tall with a very loose, weeping habit and sharp needles whorled around the stem. Its pendulous character is striking and gracious, making it an excellent specimen. Needle juniper is reliably hardy through USDA Zone 5b and must have full sun to thrive or it becomes very ratty in appearance. Tends to open up significantly with age.

J. communis var. *montana*

SHORE JUNIPER

NATIVE HABITAT

Japan

HARDINESS ZONES

USDA 6b-9, Sunset 5-9,14-15, 17, 20-24

DESCRIPTION

An evergreen ground cover, spreading to 7'-8' and reaching 1'-2' in height. Spreads 8"-12" per year. Short, sharp needles. Young plants are low-growing and dense but often develop more upright and irregular shoots with age.

GARDEN USE

An attractive, dense ground cover, especially for coastal gardens, as it has excellent salt tolerance. Cultivars are better garden plants than the species. Some retain more uniformly dense habit with age than others. In full sun, shore juniper, with its bolder texture, is a handsome alternative to other groundcover junipers. Unfortunately, it is also appealing to hungry rodents.

HOW TO GROW

Plant in full sun in a range of soils, including very sandy, maritime soils. Provide even moisture for the first two full growing seasons.

CULTIVARS AND RELATED SPECIES

'Blue Lagoon' — A selection with bright blue foliage.
'Blue Pacific' — A very flat, fresh blue-green, prostrate plant.
'Emerald Sea' — A dense ground cover with green-blue foliage.
'Silver Mist' — A very compact plant with silvery blue foliage.
'Sunsplash' — Yellow-splashed foliage.
Juniperus procumbens, Japanese Garden Juniper — A beautiful, dense ground cover with more pastel shades of gray-green foliage than other ground cover junipers.
J. procumbens 'Nana' — A popular, comparatively slow-growing selection. Traditionally used in rock gardens and for bonsai but also an excellent garden plant in general.

Juniperus conferta 'Blue Lagoon'

GROUND COVER JUNIPER

NATIVE HABITAT
Northern North America

HARDINESS ZONES
USDA 2-9(10), Sunset 1-12, 18-21

DESCRIPTION
One of our reliable, cold-hardy, native conifers. A low, evergreen, prostrate, irregularly spreading shrub less than 1' in height. Spreads 8"-12" per year, to 10'-12' with age. Scale-like leaves are held close to the stem, needle-like leaves at a wider angle to the stem. Cultivars vary significantly.

GARDEN USE
The many wonderful cultivars of *J. horizontalis* are sadly underused and could help make ground-cover plantings much more diverse. Many cultivars assume beautiful plum hues in winter. Cultivars with various textures and colors can be combined for an interesting effect.

HOW TO GROW
Plant in full sun. Tolerates a range of soils. Provide even moisture for the first growing season.

CULTIVARS AND RELATED SPECIES
'Bar Harbor' and 'Wiltonii' (frequently sold as 'Blue Rug') — Ubiquitous (but reliable) flat, blue plants.
'Blue Chip' — Has a somewhat irregular silhouette and bright, silver-blue color.
'Emerald Spreader' — Gray-green. Very dense and mat-like.
'Heidi' — Smoky, gray-green color, and unique fern-like appearance.
'Lime Glow' — Burnished gold winter color and an unusually upright, mounding habit to 18" in height.
'Mother Lode' — Very flat, pancake habit; bright yellow-gold in winter.
'Prince of Wales' — Tight habit and rich green, brushy foliage that turns a handsome purple-green in winter.
'Variegata' — Splashed lightly with creamy white.

Juniperus horizontalis

Juniperus scopulorum

ROCKY MOUNTAIN JUNIPER

NATIVE HABITAT

Rocky Mountains and adjacent areas of western North America

HARDINESS ZONES

USDA 4-7, Sunset 1-5, 8-15, 18-21

DESCRIPTION

A medium evergreen tree to over 50' in the wild, usually no more than 20' in cultivation, with a habit that varies from flame-shaped to conical to narrowly pyramidal. Grows 6"-12" per year. Leaves are very small and scale-like. Juvenile needles are held at wider angles from the stem.

GARDEN USE

Many selections have bright blue foliage and extremely narrow, "pencil point" habits. Widely used as accent and screening plants.

HOW TO GROW

Plant in full sun and well-drained soils. Provide even moisture for the first two full growing seasons. Very drought tolerant once established. Native populations of this plant range in elevation from sea level in Vancouver to over 6,000' in the Rockies, with accompanying variation in cold hardiness. A good performer in cool, dry climates but very susceptible to pests and diseases in hot, humid regions and not tolerant of very poorly drained soils. Most successful west of the Mississippi.

CULTIVARS AND RELATED SPECIES

'Moonglow' — A broad pyramid with eye-catching silver-blue foliage.
'Pathfinder' — A narrow pyramid with blue-gray foliage.
'Skyrocket' — A very narrow pyramid with powder-blue foliage.
'Tolleson's Blue Weeping' and 'Tolleson's Green Weeping' — Weeping selections with blue-gray and gray-green foliage respectively. Both are irresistible when young but tend to open up with age and lose some appeal.
'Wichita Blue' — A narrowish pyramid with bright-blue foliage.

SINGLESEED JUNIPER

NATIVE HABITAT
Himalayas, western China and the mountains of Taiwan

HARDINESS ZONES
USDA 5-8, Sunset 2-16, 18-21

DESCRIPTION
An evergreen shrub that varies in height from 6'-12', usually low and spreading in the wild. Habit varies by cultivar from low, mounding ground cover to upright, relaxed shrub. Sharp-pointed foliage is held stiffly at moderate angles from the stem.

GARDEN USE
All cultivars have moderate growth rates and are therefore easily managed in small spaces. Singleseed juniper is exceptionally tough, drought tolerant and reliable in a range of landscapes, and deserves much wider use. The foliage in handsome shades of blue is a prominent feature of the plant.

HOW TO GROW
Plant in full sun in a range of soils, from rocky gravels to sands to clays. Provide even moisture for the first full growing season.

Juniperus squamata 'Blue Star'

CULTIVARS AND RELATED SPECIES
'Blue Alps' — A lovely, narrowly vase-shaped selection with pendant branch tips and bright-blue foliage.
'Blue Star' — The most widely planted mounding selection. Bright blue foliage has a slightly softer texture than that of the species.
'Holger' — A robust, spreading, blue-gray shrub (like a narrow Pfitzer). New growth emerges frosted with gold in spring.
'Meyeri' — An old cultivar that is a large, lax shrub with bright blue foliage (and the parent of 'Blue Star').

EASTERN RED CEDAR

NATIVE HABITAT
Eastern U.S. and Canada

HARDINESS ZONES
USDA 3-10, Sunset all zones

DESCRIPTION
An evergreen, small to large tree usually 20'-50' in cultivation with variable spread. Grows 8"-12" per year. Habit of cultivars and wild seedlings varies widely. Leaves are very small and scale-like. Juvenile needles are held at wide angles from stem.

GARDEN USE
Seedling characteristics are not always stellar, but named cultivars offer tremendous beauty in a conifer native to a huge portion of the gardening U.S. Use cultivars as specimens or screens. Berry-like, blue-gray cones are highly ornamental when borne in profusion.

HOW TO GROW
A reliable performer in full sun or light shade in a range of soils. Provide even moisture for the first full growing season. There is considerable variation in cold hardiness, so purchase unnamed seedlings only when their origin is known and indicates the plant is likely to be hardy in your area.

CULTIVARS AND RELATED SPECIES
Emerald Sentinel ('Corcorcor') — Excellent winter color and tall columnar habit. Winner of the Pennsylvania Horticultural Society's Gold Medal.
'Grey Owl' — A large, spreading shrub bright silver-gray in color.
'Hillspire' — Emerald green foliage and good winter color.

Juniperus virginiana

'Pendula' — A large shrub with a weeping habit.
var. *silicicola* — The southern variant found in coastal areas of Florida and adjacent states. Virtually identical in appearance but less cold hardy than the species.
'Stover' — Narrow habit and glowing, silver-blue foliage.

EUROPEAN LARCH

Larix decidua

NATIVE HABITAT
Europe

HARDINESS ZONES
USDA 3-6, Sunset 1-9, 14-17

DESCRIPTION
A tall, deciduous conifer to 80' tall. Pyramidal when young, becoming open with age. Grows 1'-2' per year. Needles are 1" long and green to yellowish green, borne in whorls on spur shoots. Branches are arranged in horizontal whorls. Cones are 1"-1½" long, borne upright on the branches and pink, becoming brown. Bark is charcoal-gray.

GARDEN USE
Spectacular golden fall color and an interesting branch pattern in winter, followed by soft green hues in spring are a few of this plant's attractive features. Plant with a backdrop of darker evergreens to enhance the outstanding foliage color.

HOW TO GROW
Most larches grow best where summers are cool. They do not tolerate shade or air pollution. Soil should be moist and well drained. Dwarf cultivars benefit from some relief from the afternoon sun.

CULTIVARS AND RELATED SPECIES
'Pendula' — A dramatic weeping selection with nice skeletal structure in winter.
L. x *eurolepis* 'Varied Directions' — Has erratic (and often dramatic!) branching.
L. kaempferi, Japanese Larch — Fast-growing to 60' in height. Foliage is a soft, bluish green.
L. kaempferi 'Blue Rabbit' — Dwarf, narrow, conical habit with beautiful, glaucous blue foliage.
L. kaempferi 'Diane' — A small tree with contorted branches.
L. laricina, American Larch or Tamarack — To 60' in height, with light green foliage.
L. laricina 'Newport Beauty' — A very dwarf, slow-growing selection with bluish green needles.

DAWN REDWOOD

NATIVE HABITAT

China

HARDINESS ZONES

USDA 5-9, Sunset 3-10, 14-24

DESCRIPTION

A large deciduous tree to over 100' (but usually 60'-80'), with a formal, conical habit. Grows 1'-3' per year. Distinctive pointed top, horizontal branching, buttressed trunk, cinnamon-red bark and bright rusty red fall color. Grass-green, ¾"-long, soft needles are arrayed in opposite pairs along branchlets. Cones are oval, ½" long and resemble honey dippers.

GARDEN USE

Metasequoia was once thought to be extinct but was discovered in a secluded valley in China in the 1940s. It has since become a fairly popular conifer as a result of its broad adaptability and cold hardiness. Its dramatic formal habit and fall color make it an excellent specimen or grove planting. Its rapid growth rate and tolerance of wet conditions make it a good tree for many gardens and streets.

HOW TO GROW

Plant in full sun in a range of soils. Provide even moisture for the first two full growing seasons. Thrives in wet sites and sites with standing water. Will succumb to severe drought on very dry soils.

CULTIVARS AND RELATED SPECIES

There are only a few cultivars, selected for their formal habit, and not significantly different from the species.

Metasequoia glyptostroboides

SIBERIAN JUNIPER

NATIVE HABITAT

Southeastern Siberia and adjacent areas

HARDINESS ZONES

USDA Zone 2-8, Sunset all zones

DESCRIPTION

An evergreen ground-cover shrub with a feathery texture to 1' tall and spreading from 3'-10' or more. Spreads about 1' per year. Leaves are small, scale-like and in small, flattened sprays.

GARDEN USE

Unlike most ground-cover conifers, *Microbiota* tolerates shade or sun. In full sun, green summer foliage turns warm red-plum in winter; in shade, foliage stays green through the winter. Remarkably cold hardy in areas where winter temperatures do not fluctuate dramatically. Excellent informal, graceful ground cover, especially for massing across areas with changing or drastically differing light conditions. The winter color change can be used creatively in sunny winter gardens.

HOW TO GROW

Plant in full sun to full shade in a range of soils. Requires good drainage, but should not be allowed to dry out for its first two to three growing seasons. Withstands drought once established. Best in northern gardens but tolerates some heat and humidity.

CULTIVARS AND RELATED SPECIES

No cultivars are available in the U.S.

Microbiota decussata

NORWAY SPRUCE

NATIVE HABITAT

Europe

HARDINESS ZONES

USDA 3-7, Sunset 1-6, 14-17

DESCRIPTION

A large, wide-spreading tree to 100' tall by 40' wide. Grows up to 2' per year. Needles are dark green, shiny and ½"-¾" long. A brown peg remains on the twig after a leaf falls (this is true of all spruce species). Side branchlets droop with age. Cones are pendulous and 4"-6" long.

GARDEN USE

A tough, fast-growing tree useful for screening or as a specimen tree. New growth can be sheared in spring to make a hedge. This tree's fast growth rate and ease of transplanting have made it inexpensive and popular. Unfortunately, it is often planted in confined spaces, which it quickly overwhelms.

HOW TO GROW

Plant in full sun. Tolerates dry sites and windy conditions. Scale, mites, spruce gall adelgids and canker are problems, especially in warm, humid areas.

CULTIVARS AND RELATED SPECIES

There are hundreds of dwarf selections, including some of the most popular dwarf conifers.

'Acrocona' — An irregularly shaped shrub that produces long, reddish cones at the tips of its shoots.

'Columnaris' and 'Cupressina' — Both are narrower than other plants

continues on page 70

Picea abies

69

of the species, particularly 'Cupressina'. 'Columnaris' is wider and less formal in outline.
'Clanbrassiliana Stricta' — A formal cone shape.
'Gregoryana' — Very dwarf, becoming a tight bun 18" by 18".
'Maxwellii' is similar but larger.
'Hillside Upright' — A slow-growing, small, conical tree.
'Inversa' — A small weeping tree with an upright habit, gradually growing taller with age. 'Pendula' is also a weeping plant, but tends to stay low.

'Little Gem' and 'Witches' Brood' — Both tightly growing small shrubs.
'Nidiformis', Bird's Nest Spruce — A dwarf shrub, becoming 3' high and 5' wide in about 10-15 years. 'Repens' is shorter and more spreading. 'Pumila' is similar but better than the others for cold climates because it breaks bud later in the spring.

P. orientalis, Oriental Spruce — A very attractive, narrow (20' wide) tree with very short (less than ½"), dark-green needles. One of the most beautiful spruces and useful in many gardens because of its narrow spread. Also tolerates heat better than most spruces. Received the Pennsylvania Horticultural Society's Gold Medal in 1992. USDA Zones 5-7, Sunset 4-6, 14-17.

P. orientalis 'Aurea' — New growth is creamy yellow, turning dark green by mid-summer. Size is the same as the species.

P. orientalis 'Gowdy' — A dense, narrow tree with small, dark-green leaves.

P. orientalis 'Skylands' — Selected for its golden color and somewhat slower growth rate. New growth is bright yellow; old foliage appears to be brushed with gold.

Picea abies

SERBIAN SPRUCE

NATIVE HABITAT
Bosnia and Serbia

HARDINESS ZONES
USDA 4-7, Sunset 4-6, 14-17

DESCRIPTION
A narrow tree 60' tall by 20' wide, with drooping branches that turn up at the ends. Grows up to 12" per year. Needles are flat, glossy, dark green on one side and bluish on the other side, and up to 1" long. A brown peg remains on the twig after a leaf falls. Cones are pendulous and up to 2½" long.

Picea omorika

GARDEN USE
A graceful tree with two-toned needles. Attractive in groupings, for screening and as a specimen. Its narrow form makes it suitable for most gardens.

HOW TO GROW
Plant in full sun. Tolerates heat, humidity and wind. Canker and scale are occasionally problems, especially in warmer, more humid regions. Not vulnerable to snow and ice damage.

CULTIVARS AND RELATED SPECIES
'Nana' — A dwarf, broadly conical shrub with two-toned needles. 'Pendula' — A tree that grows more slowly than other plants of the species. The central leader is upright, with pendulous branches. *P. breweriana*, Brewer's Weeping Spruce — A tree with very pendulous side branches and two-toned needles. Does best in its native northwestern California and southwestern Oregon, but is difficult to find in nurseries. Requires moisture and cool temperatures. USDA Zone 5, Sunset 4-7, 14-17.

COLORADO SPRUCE

Picea pungens f. *glauca*

NATIVE HABITAT
Rocky Mountains

HARDINESS ZONES
USDA 2-6, Sunset 1-10, 14-17

DESCRIPTION
A dense, pyramidal tree 60' tall by 25' wide. Grows 6"-12" per year.

Needles are sharp, stiff, to 1½" long and green to blue in color. A brown peg remains on the twig after a leaf falls. Cones are tan, pendulous and 3"-4" long.

GARDEN USE
Selections of this species are some of the bluest of conifers. They are available in a variety of forms, from low shrubs to large trees. The silvery blue is especially attractive if used with purple foliage or pink flowers. The bluer forms tend to be slower growing. Old plants tend to lose lower branches and become unattractive.

HOW TO GROW
Plant in full sun. Tolerant of dry sites, wind, air pollution and salt. In warm, humid areas, it is very susceptible to mites, spruce gall adelgids and cankers. Winter burn can also be a problem.

CULTIVARS AND RELATED SPECIES
f. *glauca* — Bluer than other plants of the species. Same size as the species.
'Argentea', 'Fat Albert', 'Hoopsii', 'Koster' and 'Moerheim' — Silvery blue selections that grow relatively large.

'Iseli Foxtail' — New growth is blue, bushy and twisted. Form is an upright, tight cone. More heat tolerant than other plants of the species.

'Iseli Fastigiate' — A narrowly upright, blue tree.

'Montgomery' — A dwarf, silvery blue shrub that grows 3"-6" per year. 'Globosa' and 'Glauca Compacta' are similar.

P. glauca, White Spruce — An excellent large-scale spruce for cold climates, USDA Zones 2-5 (Sunset 1-6, 14-17). Leaves are bluish green.

P. glauca 'Conica', Dwarf Alberta Spruce — A dense, conical shrub with light green foliage. Becomes 3'-4' tall by 1½' wide in 10-15 years.

Often used as a container plant. Protect from reflected sunlight, hot and cold winds, but provide good air circulation. USDA Zones 5-6. 'Rainbow's End' is similar, but has creamy yellow new growth. Needs light shade to protect it from burning.

P. glauca 'Sander's Blue' — A very attractive blue form of Dwarf Alberta Spruce with the unfortunate tendency to revert to the green form.

P. glauca var. *densata*, Black Hills Spruce — This variety has heavier needles and is a smaller-scale tree than other plants of the species. It is one of the best evergreens for the Northern Plains.

P. pungens, foliage

LACEBARK PINE

NATIVE HABITAT
China

HARDINESS ZONES
USDA 5-8, Sunset 1-11, 14-24

DESCRIPTION
A beautiful tree up to 50' tall by 30' wide, often multistemmed. Grows 6"-10" per year. Young plants tend to be dense and pyramidal, but become much more open with age. Needles are stiff, dark olive-green, 2"-4" long and grow in groups of three. Cones are 2"-3" long. The bark peels.

GARDEN USE
The bark exfoliates in small flakes, becoming a patchwork of green, white and gray — hence the name lacebark pine — and gradually turns chalk white with age and exposure. Many feel this is the most attractive of the pines due to its ornamental bark. The bark starts peeling within 10 years and becomes more beautiful with age. This pine is usually used as a specimen tree to emphasize the bark.

HOW TO GROW
Plant in full sun with excellent drainage. Tolerates wind and drought. Generally healthy.

CULTIVARS AND RELATED SPECIES
No cultivars of lacebark pine are currently available.

Pinus bungeana

SWISS STONE PINE

NATIVE HABITAT
Central Europe, southwestern Asia

HARDINESS ZONES
USDA 3-6, Sunset 1-6, 14-17

DESCRIPTION
A short, narrow, slow-growing tree to 30' tall by 10' wide. Grows 4"-6" per year. Needles are bluish green, 2"-5" long and in groups of five. Cones are 2"-3" long with large, edible seeds. The thick twigs are covered with dense, brown hairs.

GARDEN USE
Useful in almost any size garden. Primarily used as a specimen, but also attractive in groups or as screening.

HOW TO GROW
Plant in full sun with excellent drainage. Tolerates wind and salt. Scale and borers can be a problem, especially in warm, humid areas. Performs well in much of the northern half of the country.

CULTIVARS AND RELATED SPECIES
'Chalet' — Becomes a dense, rounded, columnar tree.
'Columnaris' — Habit is a bit narrower than that of other plants of the species.

'Glauca' and 'Silver Sheen' — Foliage is bluer than that of other plants of the species.
'Nana' — Slower growing than other plants of the species.

Pinus cembra

P. edulis, Pinyon Pine — A small, bushy tree 15'-20' high, with 2"-long needles in clusters of two. Seeds are edible. Native to the Southwest. USDA Zones 5-8, Sunset 1-11, 14-24.
P. pinea, Italian Stone Pine, Umbrella Pine — The flat-topped "pine of Rome," which graces the hills of central Italy. Leaves grow in pairs, to 6" long. Cones are 5" long with edible seeds. Does well in California. USDA Zones 7b-9, Sunset 5-11, 13-24.

JAPANESE RED PINE

NATIVE HABITAT
Japan and Korea

HARDINESS ZONES
USDA 5-8, Sunset 1-6, 14-17

DESCRIPTION
A picturesque tree up to 60' tall by 30' wide. Single or multistemmed with horizontal branches. Grows up to 12" per year. Needles are 3"-5" long in groups of two. Cones are 1"-2" long in clusters of three to five. Attractive reddish bark.

Pinus densiflora 'Oculus-draconis'

GARDEN USE
For use in screening, as a specimen or as a street tree. Very popular for bonsai and in Japanese gardens.

HOW TO GROW
Plant in full sun with good drainage. Salt and drought tolerant. Scale, pine spittle bug and sawfly larvae may be problems.

CULTIVARS AND RELATED SPECIES
'Globosa' — A multistemmed, semi-dwarf, rounded shrub.
'Little Christopher' — Another small shrub, with a rounded, globe-like shape and bright green needles.
'Oculus-draconis', Dragon's Eye Red Pine — Each needle has two yellow bands. When viewed from above, this creates the appearance of alternating yellow and green rings. Slower growing than other trees of the species, to 20'-30' in height.
'Pendula' — A prostrate plant that makes an interesting ground cover or, when staked, an unusual sculptural form.
'Umbraculifera', Tanyosho Pine — A multistemmed, intermediate-size conifer, eventually about 20' high. Bark is exceptionally attractive.

MUGHO PINE, MOUNTAIN PINE

NATIVE HABITAT

Mountains of southern Europe

HARDINESS ZONES

USDA 3-7, Sunset 1-6, 14-17

DESCRIPTION

A multistemmed, shrubby pine growing to 15' high by 15' wide. Needles are 1"-3" long, in twos, dark green and slightly twisted. Cones are 1"-2½" long.

GARDEN USE

A picturesque shrub that can easily outgrow its allotted space. Slower-growing cultivars are better in most situations. Root-hardy in most areas and thus useful as a container plant. Plants sold are seed-grown and vary greatly in growth habit, size and needle length.

HOW TO GROW

Plant in full sun with good drainage. Tolerates low soil fertility. Problems with *Diplodia* tip blight, scale and pine shoot moths, especially in warmer, more humid areas. Does very well in the North and in non-desert areas of the West. If you want a small shrub, select an appropriate cultivar. Pruning the new shoot (candle) growth can keep plants small, but must be done every spring.

CULTIVARS AND RELATED SPECIES

P. mugo var. *mugo* — When you buy mugho pine, you usually get this variety.

P. mugo 'Mops' — A low-growing shrub. Other compact forms include 'Compacta', 'Gnom', 'Green Candle', 'Prostrata', var. 'Pumilio' and 'Sherwood Compact'.

P. mugo 'Big Tuna' — A slow-growing, upright shrub.

Pinus mugo var. *mugo,* candles

PONDEROSA PINE

NATIVE HABITAT
Western North America

HARDINESS ZONES
USDA 3-7, Sunset 1-6, 14-17

DESCRIPTION
A bold tree to 80' tall and 25' wide. Grows 8"-15" per year. Needles are 4"-10" long, green (sometimes with a slightly silver cast) and in groups of three. Cones are 3"-6" long. A very important western timber tree that can reach heights of over 200' in the wild. Also known as the western yellow pine.

Pinus ponderosa

GARDEN USE
A rugged, coarse-textured tree that is attractive as a specimen, in groupings and as a wind break. Attractive bark is deeply furrowed with irregular, yellow-brown plates.

HOW TO GROW
Plant in full sun with good drainage. Tolerates drought, wind and poor, gravelly soils. May have some fungal problems in the humid East.

CULTIVARS AND RELATED SPECIES
P. canariensis, Canary Islands Pine — A tall, fast-growing, pyramidal tree. Widely used in, and one of the best pines for, the milder areas of California. Not as susceptible to some of the pest problems that plague other species. Good street and park tree. Grows to 60'-80'. Needles are medium green, 6"-12" long, in clusters of three. Cones are 8" long. USDA Zone 9, Sunset 9, 14-24. *P. contorta*, Shore Pine — A contorted, densely branched tree growing 20' high. Leaves are in groups of two. Tends to grow best along the West Coast. USDA 5-8, Sunset 1-6, 14-17. *P. contorta* var. *latifolia*, Lodgepole

Pine — This variety grows farther inland than shore pine in mountain areas. A tall, narrow tree that may reach over 70' high.

P. contorta 'Spaan's Dwarf' — A low-growing or rounded shrub with thick, upward-pointing branches and short needles. Popular as a bonsai subject.

P. halepensis, Aleppo Pine — A dense, rounded, fast-growing tree, to 30' or more. This Mediterranean species grows well in California's coastal and desert regions. More susceptible to pests than Canary Islands pine. Needles are bright green, to 4" long, in groups of three. Cones are 3½" long. USDA Zones 8-9, Sunset 5-11, 13-24.

P. radiata, Monterey Pine — This California pine is distorted and low-growing when exposed to sea winds in its native central coastal area, but reaches 100' when protected in cultivation. Leaves are 4"-6" long in clusters of three. Cones are 3"-5" long. Hardy to 15°F. Best adapted to non-desert areas of California, where it is widely cultivated (but subject to a number of problems). USDA Zones 7b-9, Sunset 5-11, 13-24.

P. torreyana, Torrey Pine — A massive, broad, and fast-growing tree with an open habit; grows to 40'.

Needles are stiff, gray-green, in groups of five and 7"-10" long. Cones grow to 6" long. Tolerates a wide range of conditions in the southwestern U.S. USDA Zones 8-9, Sunset 5-11, 13-24.

P. ponderosa, foliage and cone

EASTERN WHITE PINE

NATIVE HABITAT
Eastern North America

HARDINESS ZONES
USDA 3-7, Sunset 1-6, 14-17

Pinus strobus

DESCRIPTION
A fast-growing, fine-textured tree that becomes graceful and picturesque with age. Grows to 80' tall by 40' wide. Can grow up to 3' per year. Needles are bluish green, soft, 3"-5" long and in groups of five. Cones are 4"-6" long.

GARDEN USE
Often used in screening, although its width and tendency to lose its lower limbs limit its usefulness. A beautiful specimen tree.

HOW TO GROW
Plant in full sun. Excellent drainage is crucial. Will not tolerate salt, air pollution or prolonged drought. Loses branches to snow and ice. In the right conditions, tends to be very healthy. Does poorly in the West.

CULTIVARS AND RELATED SPECIES
'Blue Shag' — A dwarf shrub with bluish needles.
'Fastigiata' — Columnar as a young tree, becoming wider with age. Much less likely to break with snow and ice.
'Nana' — A dwarf shrub. A catch-all name for many dwarf white pines.
'Pendula' — A very pendulous plant growing about 8'-10' tall, more with staking.
'Sea Urchin' — An extremely dwarf form, with bluish needles.
P. aristata, Bristlecone Pine — A shrub or small tree native to the mountains of southwestern U.S., where some specimens are over

4,000 years old. Needles are short, in bundles of five and have white resin dots (which can be confused with mealy bugs or aphids). Does well in cool areas of California as well as the North Central and Northeast regions. USDA Zones 4-7, Sunset 1-6, 14-17.

P. flexilis, Limber Pine — A western U.S. native similar to eastern white pine, but with thicker, more flexible branches and persistent needles (resulting in a fuller tree). More tolerant of wind and drought than *P. strobus*, but prone to disease in areas of high humidity. Tolerates very dry conditions. USDA Zones 4-7, Sunset 1-10, 14-17.

P. flexilis 'Pendula' — A prostrate ground cover with bluish needles.

P. flexilis 'Vanderwolf's Pyramid' — Narrow form. Becomes a large tree.

P. parviflora, Japanese White Pine — A tree with curved trunk and leaves. Reaches 50' high by 35' wide. Salt-tolerant. Attractive cones are 2"-4" long and persist up to six years. Grows well in the Northwest and the East, and does moderately well in the Midwest and Southwest. USDA Zones 5-8, Sunset 1-6, 14-17. The many attractive cultivars of this species include the well-known 'Glauca', with blue, twisted needles

and an abundance of cones.

P. wallichiana, Himalayan Pine — An elegant, wide-spreading tree with longer and more pendulous needles than those of *P. strobus*.

P. aristata

Grows to 80' tall by 50' wide. Cones are cylindrical and stalked, 6"-10" long. Intolerant of hot, dry conditions. USDA Zones 5-8, Sunset 1-6, 14-17.

P. wallichiana 'Zebrina' — A slow-growing tree with yellow-banded needles.

SCOTS PINE

NATIVE HABITAT
Europe and northern Asia

HARDINESS ZONES
USDA 3-8, Sunset 1-6, 14-17

DESCRIPTION
A picturesque tree that becomes flat-topped with age. Grows as tall as 60', and spreads to about 30'. Can grow as much as 12" per year. Needles grow in twos, to 3" long, and are bluish green and twisted. Showy orange bark. Cones are yellowish brown, 1"-3" long.

GARDEN USE
Useful as a specimen, in groupings and as a windbreak or screen. Root hardy in most areas and thus useful as a container plant.

HOW TO GROW
Plant in full sun with good drainage. Tolerates very low soil fertility. Very susceptible to *Diplodia* tip blight in warm, humid areas. Good air circulation is essential.

CULTIVARS AND RELATED SPECIES
'Beuvronensis' — A globose dwarf of irregular habit, growing less than 2" per year. 'Glauca Nana' is similar but bluer.

'Fastigiata' — A narrowly columnar tree, perhaps the narrowest of any pine; reaches 15'-20'. Very susceptible to ice, snow and fungal damage.

'Hillside Creeper' — A prostrate ground cover with dark green leaves. 'Albyns' and 'Repens' are also mat-forming.

'Watereri' — A round, multi-stemmed shrub or small tree that becomes flat-topped with age, quite similar to Tanyosho Pine (*P. densiflora* 'Umbraculifera').

Pinus sylvestris

LOBLOLLY PINE

NATIVE HABITAT

Southeastern United States

HARDINESS ZONES

USDA 7-9, Sunset 3-11, 13-24

DESCRIPTION

A fast-growing tree that is quite common in its native Southeast. Needles are bright green, 6"-10" long and in groups of three. Bark is reddish brown, attractive and fissured into coarse plates. Cones are 2½"-4" long. Generally grows over 1' per year.

GARDEN USE

Graceful and picturesque with age. Useful for screening, as a specimen or as a street tree.

HOW TO GROW

Plant in full sun. Tolerates poor drainage, drought and infertile soils. Generally very healthy. Large specimens may be difficult to transplant, but small trees grow quickly.

CULTIVARS AND RELATED SPECIES

P. elliottii, Slash Pine — A commonly planted tree in its native Southeast, with long (8"-10") needles in clusters of two and three, and 4"-6" long cones. Tolerates poor drainage. Relatively fast growing to 100'. USDA Zones 7-9. *P. glabra,* Spruce Pine — A medium-sized, southeastern native with yellow-green needles 3" long in clusters of two. Cones are 2½" long. Tolerates relatively poor drainage. USDA Zones 8-9.
P. palustris, Long-leaf Pine — A southeastern native, with long (to 18"), drooping needles in clusters of three. Bark is an attractive orange-brown. Cones grow to 10" long. Drought-tolerant. USDA Zones 7-9, Sunset 5-11, 13-24.

Pinus taeda

JAPANESE BLACK PINE

Popular for bonsai and in Japanese gardens.

NATIVE HABIT
Japan and Korea

HARDINESS ZONES
USDA 5-10, Sunset 1-6, 14-17

DESCRIPTION
A tree up to 50' tall by 25' wide, usually growing asymmetrically, with a curved trunk, with age. Grows up to 12" per year. Needles are stiff, 4"-6" long and in groups of two. Large buds are covered with white hairs. Cones grow to 2½" long.

GARDEN USE
Used most often along highways and seashores and in windbreaks.

HOW TO GROW
Plant in full sun with good drainage. Tolerates wind and salt. Susceptible to ice and snow damage.

CULTIVARS AND RELATED SPECIES
'Thunderhead' — A compact shrub with distinctive white buds.
P. leucodermis, Bosnian Pine — A slow-growing tree with very stiff, sharp, dark green needles (about 3" long). *P. heldreichii* is similar. USDA Zones 5-7, Sunset 1-6, 14-17.
P. nigra, Austrian Pine — Similar to Japanese Black Pine, but with a straighter trunk and resinous buds. Very susceptible to *Diplodia* tip blight in the East. Fares well in the colder areas of the West. Tolerates salt and urban conditions. USDA Zones 4-7, Sunset 1-6, 14-17.
P. nigra 'Hornbrookiana' — A dwarf shrub. 'Pygmaea' is similar.
P. resinosa, Red Pine — A northeastern U.S. native similar to Austrian Pine, but with slightly reddish bark and needles that snap when bent. USDA Zones 3-6, Sunset 1-6, 14-17.
P. resinosa 'Don Smith' — A compact shrub with a flat top.

Pinus thunbergii

BIGLEAF PODOCARP

NATIVE HABITAT

Japan

HARDINESS ZONES

USDA 8-10, Sunset 4-9, 12-24

DESCRIPTION

An evergreen shrub to tree reaching 40'-50' with age in the wild. More often seen as a large shrub in cultivation. Grows 5"-10" per year. Leaves are broad and flat. *Podocarpus* is a huge genus found primarily in the warm temperate and subtropical areas of the southern hemisphere but reaches into the northern hemisphere in a few areas. A few species are grown as garden plants in Europe, in the western U.S. and occasionally in the deep South. Most often grown in conservatories outside of the warmer areas of the South and West.

GARDEN USE

This plant's informal, shrubby habit and foliage give it a tropical appearance. It is useful for screening and as a small tree or large shrub with interesting foliage.

HOW TO GROW

Plant in light shade or full sun in areas with routine cloud cover. Thrives in moist, well-drained soils.

CULTIVARS AND RELATED SPECIES

var. *maki* — A smaller, more densely upright plant than the species.
P. gracilior — An especially graceful tree similar in character to *P. macrophyllus* but with longer, narrower leaves and less cold tolerance. USDA 9-10, Sunset 12-24.
P. nagi — A much smaller, slower-growing tree than *P. macrophyllus,* with quite broad, dark green, leathery leaves. USDA 8-10, Sunset 14-24.

Podocarpus macrophyllus

GOLDEN LARCH

NATIVE HABITAT

China

HARDINESS ZONES

USDA 5-8, Sunset 2-7, 14-17

DESCRIPTION

A deciduous tree to 70' tall with an openly pyramidal habit and irregularly spreading branches when young. Develops a rounded crown with age. Grows 6"-12" per year. Needles are flat, 1"-2" long and arranged in whorls on spur shoots noticeably longer than those of *Larix*. Fall color is orange-gold. The solitary cones are borne on the upper sides of the branches and are 2"-3" long. Bark is charcoal-gray. *Pseudolarix amabilis* is also known as *Pseudolarix kaempferi*.

GARDEN USE

For use as a specimen, in mass plantings or as a street tree. The brilliant golden fall color and interesting winter branch pattern are the plant's most salient features.

HOW TO GROW

Prefers full sun and deep, rich, soils that are moist yet well-drained. Golden larch is tolerant of many soil types except alkaline.

CULTIVARS AND RELATED SPECIES

No cultivars are readily available.

Pseudolarix amabilis

DOUGLAS-FIR

NATIVE HABITAT

Western North America

HARDINESS ZONES

USDA 4-6, Sunset 1-10, 14-17

DESCRIPTION

One of the world's largest trees, growing 80' tall (250' in the wild) by 35' wide. Grows up to 18" per year. Needles are flat, linear, to 1½" long, with two white bands on the underside. Buds are distinctively long and pointed. Cones are pendulous, with prominent, three-pronged bracts. The most important timber tree in the U.S. and a popular Christmas tree.

GARDEN USE

A rapidly growing, dark green tree. Useful for screening, as a wind break and as a specimen. Typically attractive when young, becoming less so with age.

HOW TO GROW

Plant in full sun or light shade with good drainage. Tolerates wind. Scale and spruce gall adelgids can be a problem. Intolerant of heavy clay soils. Hardiness depends on the original seed source; trees native to the Pacific Coast are much less hardy that those growing farther east. Tends to be less healthy in regions with hot, humid summers.

CULTIVARS AND RELATED SPECIES

var. *glauca* — A blue-leaved, medium-sized variety that grows more slowly and is more tolerant of cold, wind and drought.

Pseudotsuga menziesii

'Graceful Grace' — A pendulous tree with long, bluish green needles.
'Fastigiata' — A columnar tree with bluish needles and ascending branches.
'Fletcheri' — A dwarf, spreading shrub.

87

JAPANESE UMBRELLA PINE

NATIVE HABITAT

Japan

HARDINESS ZONES

USDA 6(5b)-9, Sunset 4-9, 14-24

DESCRIPTION

A large evergreen tree with a formal, pyramidal habit. Grows to over 150' in the wild, usually 20'-50' in cultivation. Grows 4"-8" per year.

Sciadopitys verticillata

Unique glossy, long, flat leaves are arranged in whorls like the ribs of an umbrella.

GARDEN USE

This conifer offers a densely formal habit and outstanding dark green foliage color and texture (in northern areas the leaves may turn dull olive-green in winter). The bark on older trees is rich mahogany and peeling. These traits plus its slow growth rate make it excellent in formal gardens. Requires a reasonably non-stressful site to look its best. In the South, provide some protection from intense sun to avoid discoloring, especially when plant is young. Received the Pennsylvania Horticultural Society's Gold Medal in 1991.

HOW TO GROW

Plant in full sun or light shade, especially in the South. Soil should be moist but well drained. Provide even moisture for the first two full growing seasons.

CULTIVARS AND RELATED SPECIES

'Aurea' — Yellow foliage and slower growth rate than the species. 'Ossorio Gold' — Deeper golden foliage than that of the species. 'Variegata' — Features a range of solid cream-yellow, green and mixed cream and green leaves. 'Wintergreen' — Selected by Professor Sidney Waxman of the University of Connecticut for improved winter color in the Northeast.

COAST REDWOOD

NATIVE HABITAT
Southwest Oregon and northwest California

HARDINESS ZONES
USDA 7-8, Sunset 4-9, 14-24

DESCRIPTION
Reaching over 300' in the wild, this evergreen is one of the world's tallest trees. In cultivation, it usually grows 60'-80' tall with a medium spread. Grows 1'-2' per year. Needles are flat and arranged in pairs along branchlets and whorled around terminal branches.

GARDEN USE
Beautiful blue-green foliage, red-brown bark, large size and unusual open habit make this a bold specimen tree. Young plants massed make lovely screens.

HOW TO GROW
Plant in full sun or light shade and moist, well-drained soils, in somewhat protected sites. Provide even moisture for the first three full growing seasons. *Sequoia* is excellent in its native range as a garden tree, given sufficient space. Performs surprisingly well in the hot Southeast, except in the worst of the clay soils, given some protection from intense sun. Not especially drought tolerant.

CULTIVARS AND RELATED SPECIES
'Albo-spica' — A rather odd selection that grows rather broad and shrubby; has white-tipped needles.
'Glauca' — A selection with especially blue foliage.
'Henderson Blue' — A relatively new cultivar with dramatic bright, powdery blue foliage.
'Prostrata' — A creeping form with blue-gray foliage.
'Soquel' — An especially handsome, emerald green selection with a uniform, pyramidal habit as a young tree.

Sequoia sempervirens

GIANT SEQUOIA, BIG TREE

NATIVE HABITAT

Southwestern Sierra Nevada mountains of California

HARDINESS ZONES

USDA 6-8, Sunset 2-9, 14-24

DESCRIPTION

A large evergreen tree to over 300' tall in the wild, usually 60'-70' in cultivation with a medium spread. Grows 6"-15" per year. Distinctive, broadly conical, characteristically uniform habit. With age, forms huge trunks to over 30' in diameter, making it well known as the earth's largest tree. Needles are gray-green and held tightly on branchlets, but radiate somewhat on older portions of the branch. Primary branches radiate horizontally from the main trunk. Bark is red-brown.

GARDEN USE

The unusual, handsome color and texture of the foliage, the red-brown bark and the characteristic uniform habit and vast girth with age make this a notable specimen tree. Very dramatic when planted in groves on large properties.

HOW TO GROW

Plant in full sun or light shade in moist, well-drained soils. Provide even moisture during the first three full growing seasons.

CULTIVARS AND RELATED SPECIES

'Aurea' — A rare selection with yellow foliage.

'Glaucum' — A selection with blue foliage and an especially narrow habit.

'Hazel Smith' — A bright-blue selection with a broadly pyramidal habit.

'Pendulum' — The most widely available selection, with a very narrow, ascending trunk eventually developing a pendant leader and pendulous side branches. Its irregularly weeping habit is somewhat surreal, hence it is sometimes called the "Dr. Seuss Tree."

Sequoiadendron giganteum

TAIWANIA, FORMOSAN REDWOOD

NATIVE HABITAT

Taiwan

HARDINESS ZONES

USDA 7-9, Sunset 4-9, 12-24

DESCRIPTION

A large evergreen tree to over 150' tall in the wild, usually 40'-80' in cultivation, with a softly pyramidal outline and medium spread. Grows 8"-12" per year. Needles are sharp-pointed and sickle-shaped. Foliage retains a beautiful blue-green bloom in shaded and protected sites.

GARDEN USE

Taiwania's graceful pyramidal habit with somewhat pendant branchlets form an unusual silhouette. It is a beautiful specimen tree. Tolerance of heat, heavy clay soils and poor drainage make it a good alternative to other conifers in these kinds of sites.

HOW TO GROW

Plant in full sun or light shade in a range of soils. Provide even moisture for the first two full growing seasons. Does not keep good color in exposed, windy sites in winter and should be located accordingly.

T. cryptomerioides, foliage

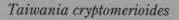

Taiwania cryptomerioides

CULTIVARS AND RELATED SPECIES

Taiwania is also found growing in China. These mainland populations are sometimes called *T. flousiana,* but whether they are significantly different from *T. cryptomerioides* remains to be decided. No cultivars are available.

BALD-CYPRESS

NATIVE HABITAT
Southeastern United States

HARDINESS ZONES
USDA 5-8, Sunset 1-9, 14-24

Taxodium distichum

DESCRIPTION
A deciduous conifer usually tall and narrow with a rounded top, to 80'. Grows 8"-15" per year. Produces woody "knees" in poorly drained sites. Needles are ½" long and medium green, turning copper in the fall. Bark is gray and peeling, with patches of orange. Cones are round, 1" in diameter and shatter when ripe.

GARDEN USE
Useful as a specimen or in a mass planting. Particularly nice when planted alongside a pond or body of water. Excellent fall color, typically copper to deep orange.

HOW TO GROW
Prefers full sun and moist acidic soils. Will tolerate drier soils and windy sites. Matted surface roots and tap root prevent the plant from being easily transplanted.

CULTIVARS AND RELATED SPECIES
var. *imbricarium*, Pond Cypress — A tree to 90' with interesting leaves that are tightly pressed against the ascending branchlets. Native to the extreme southeastern U.S. on wet, poorly drained sites and along waterways. Also known as *T. ascendens* and *T. distichum* var. *nutans*. USDA Zones 6-10, Sunset 5-9,14-24.
var. *imbricarium* 'Prairie Sentinel', Prairie Sentinel Pond Cypress — A narrow, columnar tree with horizontal branches. The original tree is 60' tall by 10' wide.
T. mucronatum, Montezuma Cypress — Wide-spreading, large evergreen tree (deciduous in colder regions) native to Mexico. Grows best with ample moisture. Grows 75' tall. USDA Zones 9-10, Sunset 8-10,12-14.

ENGLISH YEW

NATIVE HABITAT

Europe, northern Africa, Asia Minor, Caucasus

HARDINESS ZONES

USDA 6-8, Sunset 3-9, 14-24

DESCRIPTION

A small tree to 30', with wide-spreading branches and a broad crown. Grows 12"-18" per year. Needles are borne in v-shaped rows on spreading shoots and spirally arranged on erect shoots. They are ½"-1½" long and glossy, dark-green above and paler underneath. Seed is in a fleshy, red aril borne only on female plants. Bark is reddish brown and exfoliating. Foliage and seeds are poisonous.

GARDEN USE

Use as a small tree or hedge or for screening; many dwarf and columnar cultivars available. One of the few conifers that will grow in the shade. Its rich, deep-green foliage withstands shearing and pruning.

HOW TO GROW

Can grow in full sun or shade but may occasionally burn in the strong winter sun and wind if the temperatures dip too low. Prefers a moist

Taxus baccata

yet well-drained soil with a pH that is close to neutral. When pruned hard, can resprout from old wood.

CULTIVARS AND RELATED SPECIES

'Adpressa' — A dense, wide-spreading shrub to 6' tall with short needles, rounded at the tips. A female clone.

continues on page 94

'Fastigiata Robusta' — An upright, narrowly columnar shrub. Needles are coarse and medium green.

'Repandens' — Dwarf and low-growing, this popular cultivar is a female clone, with glossy, dark green foliage and low, horizontal branches that droop at the tips. Becomes 6' high and 15' wide at maturity. A bit hardier than the species.

T. cuspidata, Japanese Yew — More cold tolerant than English yew and a little more compact and shrub-like in habit, but still becomes a small tree. Needles are shorter than those of English yew, and the overall color is a rich dark green. USDA Zones 4-7, Sunset 1-6,14-17.

T. cuspidata 'Aurescens' — A dwarf, slow-growing, compact selection with bright yellow needles year-round.

T. cuspidata 'Nana' — A very old selection with a dense, mounded habit and dull, dark green needles.

T. x media, Anglojapanese Yew — A hybrid between *T. baccata* and *T. cuspidata*, with an intermediate habit. Hardiness is somewhere between those of the parents as well.

T. x media 'Densiformis' — A vigorous, free-branching selection that remains dense without shearing. This male clone is bright green.

T. x media 'Everlow' — A wide, low-spreading and moderately vigorous male clone. A good low-growing yew.

T. x media 'Hatfieldii' — A selection with a broadly upright to pyramidal habit that grows to 10' or more. Needles are rather broad, leathery and glossy, dark green. Another male clone.

T. x media 'Hicksii', Hick's Yew — An upright, female selection that becomes broader with age. The needles are long and dark, lustrous green.

T. baccata, foliage and seeds

EASTERN ARBORVITAE

NATIVE HABITAT

Northeastern North America and mountainous areas of the southeastern United States

HARDINESS ZONES

USDA Zone 2-8, Sunset 2-9, 15-17

DESCRIPTION

A medium evergreen tree to 50' in the wild, usually 10'-30' in cultivation with a variable spread. Grows 8"-12" per year. Habit and growth rate vary according to cultivar. Upright, flattened sprays of green to gray-green foliage. A staple of the nursery and landscape trade that has been in cultivation since the 1500s.

GARDEN USE

Exceptionally useful for screening, as it is naturally narrow, remains branched to the ground and tolerates shearing. Winter performance varies greatly by selection; some bronze quite heavily in winter while others retain better color.

HOW TO GROW

Plant in full sun or light shade in a range of soils, except extremely poorly drained clay. Reliable in a range of northern sites, but much shorter lived in hot, humid climates.

Thuja occidentalis 'Rheingold'

Provide even moisture for the first two full growing seasons. Look for single-leader plants where possible to avoid ice damage and related problems with age.

CULTIVARS AND RELATED SPECIES

There are over 100 cultivars, and *continues on page 96*

improved selections come into production all the time.

'Aurea' — A tree with yellow-gold foliage.

'DeGroot Spire' — A cultivar with fine texture and a very narrow, columnar habit.

'Emerald Green' (also listed as 'Smaragd') — Has a uniformly narrow habit, bright emerald green foliage, excellent winter color and improved heat tolerance.

'Hetz Midget' and 'Tiny Tim' — Two rounded, very dwarf selections.

'Nigra' — A tall, narrow plant with dark green foliage and good winter color.

'Pendula' — A weeping plant that slowly becomes a large shrub.

'Rheingold' — A slow-growing shrub with gold-bronze juvenile foliage.

'Sherwood Moss' — Has a rounded habit and juvenile (needle-like) gray-green foliage.

'Spiralis' — A small tree with glaucous, gray-green to blue-green, slightly fern-like foliage with a unique and handsome texture.

'Sunkist' — A selection with yellow foliage and an especially conical habit.

'Techny' — A standard-sized tree with dark green foliage.

'Wansdyke Silver' — A cultivar with silver-white frosted foliage and branch tips.

Thuja occidentalis 'Emerald Green'

ORIENTAL ARBORVITAE

NATIVE HABITAT

Eastern Asia

HARDINESS ZONES

USDA 6(5b)-10, Sunset 2-9, 13-16, 18-22

DESCRIPTION

A small, often multistemmed, evergreen tree to over 30' in the wild, usually 8'-15' in cultivation. Grows 8"-12" per year. Habit varies by cultivar but is generally a uniform, rounded conical shape that opens somewhat with age. Very erect, flattened sprays of bright green foliage. This species is also known as *Platycladus orientalis* and as *Biota orientalis*.

GARDEN USE

Its small size and bright foliage have made this a widely used plant, especially in the South where it is more heat tolerant than *T. occidentalis*. The winter color of many selections changes to handsome shades of plum or bronze — or drab browns.

HOW TO GROW

Plant in full sun or light shade in a range of soils, including very light sands and gravels. Provide even moisture for the first full growing season. Avoid sites that flood regu-larly and areas with heavy bagworm infestations.

CULTIVARS AND RELATED SPECIES

'Bonita' — A dwarf with gold-yellow/chartreuse foliage. To 3'-5'. 'Conspicua' (often sold as 'Aurea Nana') — A selection with lime green foliage that grows about 4' tall. 'Juniperoides' — A selection with a rounded dwarf habit reaching 3'-4'. Needles are soft and steel blue, turning an attractive deep plum in winter. 'Sanderi' — A dwarf cultivar with a rounded to broadly conical habit. Thick, relatively stiff, needle-like leaves, blue-gray in summer and bright plum to red-purple in winter. ('Sanderi' and 'Juniperoides' are routinely confused in nurseries).

Thuja orientalis, golden cultivar

WESTERN ARBORVITAE, WESTERN RED CEDAR

NATIVE HABITAT
Pacific Northwest and Rocky Mountains

HARDINESS ZONES
USDA 5-9, Sunset 1-9, 14-24

DESCRIPTION
A large evergreen tree to over 150' in the wild, usually 40'-80' in cultivation, with an informal pyramidal habit and medium spread. Grows 8"-18" per year. Pendant, flattened sprays of rich green foliage.

GARDEN USE
Its rapid growth rate, handsome habit and good winter color make this a good candidate for tall hedges and screens.

Thuja plicata

HOW TO GROW
Plant in full sun in a range of soils. Provide even moisture for the first two full growing seasons.

CULTIVARS AND RELATED SPECIES
'Atrovirens' — A cultivar with a uniform habit and good winter color.
'Cuprea' — A selection with a dwarf, rounded pyramidal habit becoming more rounded with age, and foliage in shades of yellow.
'Hillieri' — Has a dwarf, rounded habit.
'Semperaurescens' — A full-sized selection with new growth that emerges yellow and fades to lime-green in summer.
'Stoneham Gold' — A large plant with bright gold edges on the leaves and branchlets and a moderate growth rate.
'Sunshine' — Has bright yellow-gold foliage that holds throughout the year.
'Zebrina' — New growth emerges deep yellow and fades to green in summer heat ('Zebrina Extra Gold' is a variant of 'Zebrina' with more gold in the leaves).
Thuja 'Green Giant' — An extraordinarily fast-growing hybrid that thrives in a range of soils and has an excellent, uniform habit, as well as good winter color.

HIBA ARBORVITAE

NATIVE HABITAT
Japan

HARDINESS ZONES
USDA 6-9, Sunset 3-7, 14-17

DESCRIPTION
An evergreen rounded shrub to tall tree eventually reaching 100' in the wild. In cultivation, usually a low, rounded shrub for many years before developing a leader and achieving significant height. Grows 4"-8" per year. Flattened sprays of bright-green, glossy, scale-like foliage with unusually broad, bright white markings on the undersides.

GARDEN USE
Makes an excellent low evergreen mass in shady sites.

HOW TO GROW
Plant in full sun to medium shade in a range of soils. Provide even moisture for the first two full growing seasons. At the northerly limit of cold hardiness for this plant, foliage consistently bronzes and burns in winter then recovers in the summer, but the plant thrives nonetheless. To prevent foliar burn in summer, variegated selections need shade as well.

CULTIVARS AND RELATED SPECIES
var. *hondai* — A small-leaved, compact form found in the wild in northern Japan.
'Nana' — A confused complex of clones often with more slender branchlets than the species. Retains a low, shrubby habit for many years, but will eventually develop a leader.
'Variegata' — Eventually a large shrub. Foliage is speckled with cream.

Thujopsis dolabrata

JAPANESE TORREYA

NATIVE HABITAT

Japan

HARDINESS ZONES

USDA 6-9, Sunset 4-23

DESCRIPTION

Similar to yew in habit, Japanese torreya grows to 30', becoming broadly pyramidal with age. Grows 6"-12" per year. Needles are borne in a horizontal plane and are ¾"-1" long with sharply pointed tips. Foliage is dark green, with two white bands beneath and very aromatic when crushed. Stems are green at first then become brown. Seeds are fleshy, about 1"-1¼" long.

Torreya nucifera

GARDEN USE

One of this tree's nicest features is its foliage — a handsome, dense, glossy dark-green in color and coarse in texture. Can be used as a single specimen or as a backdrop to other plants.

HOW TO GROW

Choose a spot with full sun or partial shade and moist, well-drained soil. Avoid strong winter winds.

CULTIVARS AND RELATED SPECIES

'Prostrata' — A low, horizontal-spreading selection.

T. californica, California Nutmeg — A tree to 40', native to cooler, shaded canyons in the California mountains. Often cultivated along the Pacific Coast. USDA Zones 8-10, Sunset 7-9, 14-24.

T. taxifolia, Florida Torreya — One of the few American conifers listed on the endangered species list, this small tree is native to Florida and Georgia along the Apalachicola River. Most of the stands have declined because of a fungal disease, and conservation efforts are underway to save and revitalize the remaining populations.

CANADA HEMLOCK, EASTERN HEMLOCK

NATIVE HABITAT

Eastern North America

HARDINESS ZONE

USDA 3-6, Sunset 3-7, 17

DESCRIPTION

An evergreen tree that grows 80' by 35' wide. Grows up to 12" per year. Needles are short, flat, ½" long, dark green above and whitish below, and borne in a flat plane. Cones ½"-¾" long, barely open when ripe. The central leader is pendulous.

GARDEN USE

A beautiful, deep green tree that thrives in both shade and sun. When healthy, the best conifer for shade and useful for screening, as a specimen and as a clipped hedge.

HOW TO GROW

Plant in full sun or shade with good drainage. Grows best in cool, rich, moist soils. Severely afflicted with scale, woolly adelgids and mites in much of the East. Smaller cultivars are easier to spray for control of insects and mites. In the Midwest, requires shelter from winter sun and wind.

CULTIVARS AND RELATED SPECIES

'Bennett' — An attractive, spreading shrub. Reaches 2' tall by 3' wide in 10-15 years.
'Cole's Prostrate' — Forms a circular, flat mat, often with an open center.

Tsuga canadensis

'Gentsch White' — A round shrub with creamy white new foliage.
'Pendula', Sargent's Weeping Hemlock — A weeping shrub, becoming a dome with age. Reaches 3' tall by 7' wide in 10 years.
T. caroliniana, Carolina Hemlock —
continues on page 102

A smaller tree native to the southern Appalachian Mountains, with leaves radiating around the stem. Cones are longer and more open than those of Canada hemlock. Tolerates hotter conditions but is still susceptible to insects and mites. USDA Zones 5-7, Sunset 3-7, 17.

T. caroliniana 'LaBar Weeping' — A pendulous, prostrate, slow-growing plant.

T. chinensis, Chinese Hemlock — This species, which looks similar to Canada hemlock, is rare in this country, but appears to be resistant to woolly adelgid and scale. USDA Zones 5-7, Sunset 3-7, 17 (has not been tested in many gardens).

T. diversifolia, Japanese Hemlock —

A naturally compact tree, rarely growing over 30' tall in American gardens. Leaves radiate from the stem, exposing their white undersides. USDA Zones 5-7, Sunset 3-7, 17.

T. heterophylla, Western Hemlock — A tall tree with dark-green needles, longer and more spreading than *T. canadensis*. Grows best along the West Coast. USDA Zone 6, Sunset Zones 1-7, 14-17.

T. mertensiana, Mountain Hemlock — A medium to tall tree with bluish, spreading needles. Grows best in cool areas of the West Coast. USDA Zone 6, Sunset Zones 1-7, 14-17.

T. mertensiana 'Elizabeth' — A spreading dwarf twice as wide as high, with beautiful blue needles.

Tsuga canadensis, cones and foliage

FOR MORE INFORMATION

The following organizations attract conifer enthusiasts (also known as coniferophytes, coneheads and pine nuts). Both sponsor national and regional meetings, tours and seed exchanges and publish journals:

American Conifer Society (ACS)
P.O. Box 360
Keswick, VA 22947-0360
Phone/Fax: (804)984-3660

North American Rock
Garden Society (NARGS)
P.O. Box 67
Millwood, NY 10546

FURTHER READING

Two of the most complete books on conifers:

Krussmann, Gerd
Manual of Cultivated Conifers
Timber Press, 1985

van Gelderen, D.M. and van Hoey Smith, J.R.P.
Conifers, The Illustrated Encyclopedia
Timber Press, 1996

Also useful and comprehensive:

Ouden, P. Den and Boom, B.K.
Manual of Cultivated Conifers
Martinus Nijhoff, 1965

Flora of North America Editorial Committee
Flora of North America
Volume 2

Oxford University Press, 1993

Good regional guides:

Cope, Edward
Native and Cultivated Conifers of Northeastern North America
Cornell University Press, 1986

Editors of Sunset Books and Sunset Magazine
The Sunset Western Garden Book
Sunset Publishing, 1995

Flint, Harrison
Landscape Plants for Eastern North America
John Wiley & Sons, 1993

Odenwald, Neil and Turner, James
Identification and Use of Southern Plants
Claitor's Publishing, 1987

Whitcomb, Carl
Know It and Grow It II
Lacebark Publications, 1983
Useful for the southcentral U.S.

More useful books:

Cutler, Sandra McLean
Conifers Coming of Age
Barton-Bradley Crossroads Publishing, 1997
A guide to mature garden conifers

Obrizok, Robert
A Garden of Conifers
Capability's Books, 1993
A descriptive checklist

Welch, Humphrey and Haddow, Gordon
The World Checklist of Conifers
Landsman's Bookshop Ltd., 1993
A listing of accepted names of species and cultivars

NURSERY SOURCES

Where to buy good plants can be a challenge. The best place to start is with local and regional nurseries and garden centers. In addition to having plants available for immediate inspection and purchase, they have staff who can answer questions about growing plants locally.

However, for less common plants it's often necessary to buy from mail-order sources as well as plant society and public garden sales. The following is a list of retail mail-order companies, many of which charge a small fee for their catalogs. This list is by no means complete and is not an endorsement of these companies nor a criticism of any not mentioned. *The Andersen Horticultural Library's Source List of Plants and Seeds* (1996, University of Minnesota) is an excellent listing of sources for individual plants.

Aesthetic Gardens
(via Internet)
http://www.agardens.com

Camellia Forest Nursery
125 Carolina Forest
Chapel Hill, NC 27516
(919) 967-5529
Catalog, $2

Coenosium Gardens
4412 354th St. East
Eatonville, WA 98328
(360) 832-8655
Catalog, $3

Dave's Nursery
234 Willow Avenue
Pompton Lakes, NJ 07422
(201) 839-6390
Free catalog

Dilworth Nursery
1200 Election Road
Oxford, PA 19363
(610) 932-0347
Free price list

Forestfarm
990 Tetherow Road
Williams, OR 97544
(541) 846-7269
Catalog, $4

Girard Nurseries
PO Box 428
Geneva, OH 44041
(216) 466-2881
Free catalog

Greer Gardens
1280 Goodpasture Island Rd
Eugene, OR 97401
(541) 686-8266
Catalog, $3 good for 2 brochures/yr
for 3 yrs

Heronswood Nursery
7530 NE 288th Street
Kingston, WA 98346
(360) 297-4172
Catalog, $4

Plant Delights Nursery
9241 Sauls Rd.
Raleigh, NC 27603
(919) 772-4794
Catalog, 10 stamps or a box of
chocolates

Porterhowse Farms
41370 SE Thomas Rd.
Sandy, OR 97055
(503) 668-5834
Catalog, $6 refundable with purchase

Rich's Foxwillow Pines Nursery
11618 McConnell Road
Woodstock, IL 60098
(815) 338-7442
Free catalog

Roslyn Nursery
211 Burrs Lane
Dix Hills, NY 11746
(516) 643-9347
Catalog, $3

Shepherd Hill Farm
200 Peekskill Hollow Road
Putnam Valley, NY 10579
(914) 528-5917
Free catalog

Stanley and Sons
11740 SE Orient Drive
Boring, OR 97009
(503) 663-4391
Free catalog

Suncrest Gardens
816 Holly Pike
Mt. Holly Springs, PA 17065
(717) 486-5142
Free catalog

Woodlanders
1128 Colleton Avenue
Aiken, SC 29801
(803) 648-7522
Catalog, $2

Yucca Do Nursery
PO Box 450
Waller, TX 77484
(409) 826-4580
Catalog, $4/2 yr

CONTRIBUTORS

SCOTT AKER is Integrated Pest Management (IPM) Coordinator at the U.S. National Arboretum, in Washington, DC.

RICHARD L. BITNER is a physician anesthesiologist and a teaching assistant in the Longwood Gardens Continuing Education Program, Kennett Square, Pennsylvania.

RONALD O. DETERMANN is the Fuqua Conservatory Superintendent at the Atlanta Botanical Garden, in Atlanta, Georgia.

GREG GRANT is the Cherokee County Horticulturist for the Texas Agricultural Extension Service. He is co-author of *The Southern Heirloom Garden*. He lives in Jacksonville, Texas.

EDWARD R. HASSELKUS is Curator of the Longenecker Horticultural Gardens at the University of Wisconsin Arboretum and is Professor Emeritus at the University of Wisconsin-Madison.

PAT HAYWARD is a sales and marketing representative for Iseli Nursery, Inc., in Boring, Oregon. She is a regular contributor to *American Nurseryman* and specializes in conifers for the West and Southwest.

JUNE HUTSON is Outdoor Project Coordinator for the Kemper Center Home Demonstration Gardens at Missouri Botanical Garden, St. Louis, Missouri. Her previous position at the garden was Curator of the Temperate Conservatory, Rock Garden and Conifer Collection.

JEFF LYNCH is Nursery Manager and a teaching assistant at Longwood Gardens in Kennett Square, Pennsylvania. He gardens in Landenberg, Pennsylvania.

SUSAN F. MARTIN has been Curator of Conifers at the U.S. National Arboretum, in Washington, DC. since 1979. She is a founding member of the American Conifer Society and a former editor of its quarterly bulletin.

ELIZABETH MCCLINTOCK is Associate Editor of and regular contributor to *Pacific Horticulture*. Her books include *An Annotated Checklist of Ornamental Plants of Coastal Southern California, An Annotated Checklist of Woody Ornamental Plants of California, Oregon and Washington, Supplement to Arizona Flora* and *Poisonous Plants of California*. She lives in San Francisco, California.

KATHY MUSIAL is Curator of Living Collections at The Huntington Botanical Gardens, San Marino, California. She has studied and collected conifers and other plants in Australia, New Zealand, Chile and Taiwan.

BRUCE STEWARD is a pest control research and marketing coordinator for the Bayer Corporation and formerly the Integrated Pest Management Coordinator at Longwood Gardens in Kennett Square, Pennsylvania.

R. WILLIAM THOMAS is Education Division Manager at Longwood Gardens, where he teaches several classes on woody plants, including conifers. He is past president of the American Conifer Society and editor of *Trees and Shrubs* (Hearst Books, 1992).

KIM TRIPP is the Director of The Botanic Garden of Smith College, Northampton, Massachusetts, and Associate for Research at the Arnold Arboretum of Harvard University in Jamaica Plain, Massachusetts. Previously, she was Curator of Conifers at the North Carolina State University Arboretum. She is co-author of *The Year in Trees* (Timber Press, 1995).

ILLUSTRATION CREDITS

R. WILLIAM THOMAS: pages 20 left and right, 22, 26, 32, 40, 41, 42 left and right, 43 top and bottom, 44, 48, 50, 53, 54, 56, 59, 60, 63, 65, 66, 70, 71, 73, 74, 75, 77, 82, 83, 88, 91 left, 98, and 99.

ALAN L. DETRICK: cover, pages 1, 25, 31, and 67.

JERRY PAVIA: pages 4, 13, 19, 21, 47, 64, 69, 80, and 96.

JOANNE PAVIA: 79.

SUSAN F. MARTIN: pages 7 left, 15, 30, 49, 51, 52, 55, 57, 61, 68, 76, and 91 right.

CHRISTINE M. DOUGLAS: pages 7 right, 18, 23, 45, 46, 58, 81, 85, 97, and 101.

GREG GRANT: page 62.

PAMELA HARPER: page 78, 84, 87, 92, 93, 94, 95, and 102.

MICHAEL DIRR: page 86 and 100.

DEREK FELL: pages 14, 17, 27, 28, 29, 72, 89, and 90.

INDEX

Brooklyn Botanic Garden
21st-Century Gardening Series

BROOKLYN BOTANIC GARDEN

NATIVE PERENNIALS

North American Beauties

21ST-CENTURY GARDENING SERIES

BROOKLYN BOTANIC GARDEN

TANTALIZING TOMATOES

Smart Tips & Tasty Picks for Gardeners Everywhere

BROOKLYN BOTANIC GARDEN

SALAD GARDENS

Gourmet Greens and Beyond

BROOKLYN BOTANIC GARDEN

BULBS FOR INDOORS

Year-round Windowsill Splendor

BROOKLYN BOTANIC GARDEN

NATURAL INSECT CONTROL

The Ecological Gardener's Guide to Foiling Pests

For further information please contact the Brooklyn Botanic Garden
1000 Washington Avenue   Brooklyn, New York 11225   (718) 622-4433 ext. 265   www.bbg.org

Watch our garden grow in your very own mailbox!

From Great Neck to Great Bend, Big River to Little Creek, over 20,000 people in all 50 states enjoy the bountiful benefits of membership in the **Brooklyn Botanic Garden** – including our renowned gardening publications.

Brooklyn Botanic Garden Membership

The splendor that makes the Brooklyn Botanic Garden one of the finest in the world can be a regular part of your life. BBG membership brings you subscriptions to some of the liveliest, best-researched, and most practical gardening publications anywhere – including the next entries in our acclaimed 21st-Century Gardening Series (currently published quarterly). BBG publications are written by expert gardeners and horticulturists, and have won prestigious *Quill and Trowel* awards for excellence in garden publishing.

SUBSCRIBER $35
(Library and Institution Rate $60)

- A full year of *21st-Century Gardening Series* handbooks
- A year's subscription to *Plants & Gardens News*
- Offerings of Signature Seeds, handbooks and videos
- Reciprocal privileges at botanical gardens across the country

Plants & Gardens News – practical tips and suggestions from BBG experts.

FAMILY/DUAL $50

All benefits of SUBSCRIBER, plus

- Membership card for free admission for two adult members and their children under 16
- 10% discount at the Terrace Cafe & Garden Gift Shop
- Free parking for four visits
- Discounts on classes, trips and tours

SIGNATURE $125

All benefits of FAMILY, plus

- Your choice of a Signature Plant from our annual catalog of rare and unique shrubs, perennials and house plants
- Unlimited free parking
- A special BBG gift calendar

BBG Catalog – quarterly listing of classes, workshops and tours in the U.S. and abroad, all at a discount.

SPONSOR $300

All benefits of SIGNATURE, plus

- Your choice of <u>two</u> Signature Plants
- Four complimentary one-time guest passes
- Invitations to special receptions

GARDENING BOOKS FOR THE NEXT CENTURY

Brooklyn Botanic Garden's 21st-Century Gardening Series explore frontiers of ecological gardening - offering practical, step-by-step tips on creating environmentally sensitive and beautiful gardens for the 1990s and the new century.

Fall 1997
Please send in this form or contact BBG
for current membership information, higher levels and benefits.

21st-Century Gardening Series – the next handbooks in this acclaimed library.